I0063956

KEEP YOUR PIE FRESH

TODD A. HESKETT

Published through Watermarq

Watermarq has been supporting organizations manage and develop their talent since 2001

Watermarq's coaching program unlocks people's potential.

For more information contact Todd directly at:
Todd.Heskett@Watermarq-Consulting.com

Copyright © 2018 Todd A. Heskett

All illustrations © 2018 Alece Birnbach
All rights reserved.

Dedications

To Hilary, my wife, my friend, and the wonderful mother
of our children. You have always been a supporter of productive
conversations and of making things happen. During my quest to
finish this book, you were tireless in supporting me while I wrote.
In return, tonight I'll make dinner, do the dishes,
and make you a cup of tea.
Love, Hub xxoo

Next, to Callum and Collette. The underlying messages
of this book are ones you've been hearing for years.
Long may they add to your continued successes.
Love, Dad xoxo

Finally, to you, the reader. You are reading this book for a reason.
I hope the value you find in its pages delivers an ROI that's
compounded exponentially beyond the
time you invest in reading its message.
Yours truly, Todd

Acknowledgements

Martin Street – for giving me the opportunity to develop Success PIE, for his team all those years ago, and for the light-hearted chiding to finish this book.

Grant Carpenter – for always being there, for being interested, and for being a friend that relentlessly gives. The value he added by brainstorming ideas and sharing his wisdom is difficult to express.

Angela Rose – for getting me through the tough bits, for being grammatically correct, and for helping straighten the strands of spaghetti, which were my initial thoughts.

Alece Birnbach – for bringing to life key messages through illustrations, and for creating characters mimicking the challenging, fun, and interesting global people that represent my clients.

Hilary Pawsey – for giving me time, space and encouragement to dream, write, and finish this book.

A Note From the Author

Welcome to *Keep Your PIE Fresh*. Here's insight into the book's background and how it's constructed to help you maximize the value you extract, based on your learning style. After all, as a wise man once told me when I began writing this book, when you go to the grocery store, you don't necessarily go down every aisle to find what you need!

- If you like getting straight to the point, read the last two pages of each chapter beginning with Chapter 1.

- If you are a visual learner, skim the book for illustrations, as they emphasize the main points of each chapter.

- If you enjoy a story that brings the main points to life, savor each word, as the characters are based on real people and real conversations – names have been changed to protect privacy.

My wish for you, is that this book inspires you to do things slightly differently to get better results and to challenge the status quo. In my subtle way, I'm trying to lead by example by starting with Chapter 0 instead of Chapter 1.

 I hope you enjoy your journey to greater success!

Warm regards,

Todd

Contents

CHAPTER 0

PIE - IT'S NOT ABOUT BAKING!

**"Genius is one percent inspiration,
ninety-nine percent perspiration."**

Thomas Edison, spoken statement (c. 1903)
Published in *Harper's Monthly* (September 1932)

"Well, that isn't something you see everyday," the café owner thought as she watched the man enter through the front door of Café Creo Prosperitas (Latin for Café Create Prosperity) and approach a group in the corner.

Though clad in a colorful spandex top, he couldn't be a runner. While the café owner often served them this time of day, as they refueled on caffeine and gluten-free organic muffins after their early morning workouts, runners never wore suits, and this gentleman was sporting one in natty brown tweed.

Runners also didn't wear capes, but she was almost certain she saw red fabric billowing behind him as he walked. She looked again. Yes, that's definitely a cape, she thought, also noting the large sketchbook the man had tucked beneath his arm. She called a barista from the back to take over at the counter so she could move closer to the group in the corner. She had to find out what this guy was up to.

"Hi, folks!" exclaimed the uniquely outfitted gentleman as he set his sketchbook on a table and gave a quick twirl to display the brilliant gold P, I, and E emblazoned across the back of his cape and the front of his shirt.

"I'm the PIE Guy," he said with a laugh, "but you probably already knew that. If you're waiting in this corner of the café, you must be here for this week's group coaching session. It's a gorgeous day today, so if you've finished your coffee and muffins, let's head outside and turn this into a walk-and-talk while I introduce you to the concept of PIE."

"Ahem…" The café owner quietly cleared her throat, hoping to attract the attention of the fascinating fellow before her.

The PIE Guy turned and smiled. "Well, good morning!" he bellowed jovially. "Would you like to join us?" he said, extending his hand.

The café owner extended hers as well. As they shook she said, "Thanks for the offer, but I already know how to bake. The muffins everyone ordered this morning are a personal recipe, made fresh every morning. I was just intrigued by your outfit and wondered what kind of pie you were talking about baking."

The PIE Guy smiled and grabbed his sketchbook, whipping it open to the first page. On it was written:

PIE

It's not
about baking!

"I get that a lot," he laughed. "This is actually a group coaching meeting, where our focus is creating greater success at work." He continued flipping to another page, which read "PIE = Preparedness, Image, and Effort: It's a recipe for achieving greater success at work."

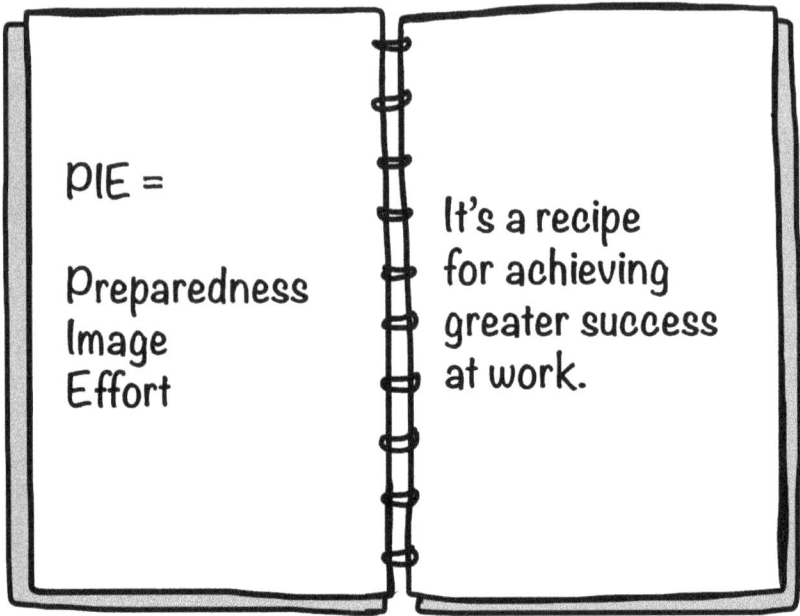

PIE =

Preparedness
Image
Effort

It's a recipe
for achieving
greater success
at work.

"PIE helps when people are looking for a better career trajectory or if they want to achieve something greater than their current situation at work. Some people are changing roles, careers, or companies and want to ensure they have the best possible start. This is where PIE helps. Today's business is full of change, pressures, 'fire fighting' and last-minute requests. Simply working harder isn't enough anymore. If you want to achieve extraordinary results, you need to change the way you work—it's essential. For this reason, you need to learn new strategies to help you become more productive and get better results."

The café owner said, "This sounds interesting and I can see that you are passionate about the topic, but how does PIE create greater success for me?"

"I believe that personal development alters our success. I have a little motto to help people understand where PIE fits into personal development and how we can achieve greater success at work." As he flipped the page in his sketchbook, this time it read "Development ALTERS Success." And in finer print below, "ALTERS = Act. Learn. Think. Elevate. Repeat. Share." The PIE Guy explained, "When we begin the journey of learning, we accelerate our success faster than by allowing it to take place naturally over time. By actively engaging in learning, we alter our success, whereby A.L.T.E.R.S. is the process of learning and growing. In short, development alters success when

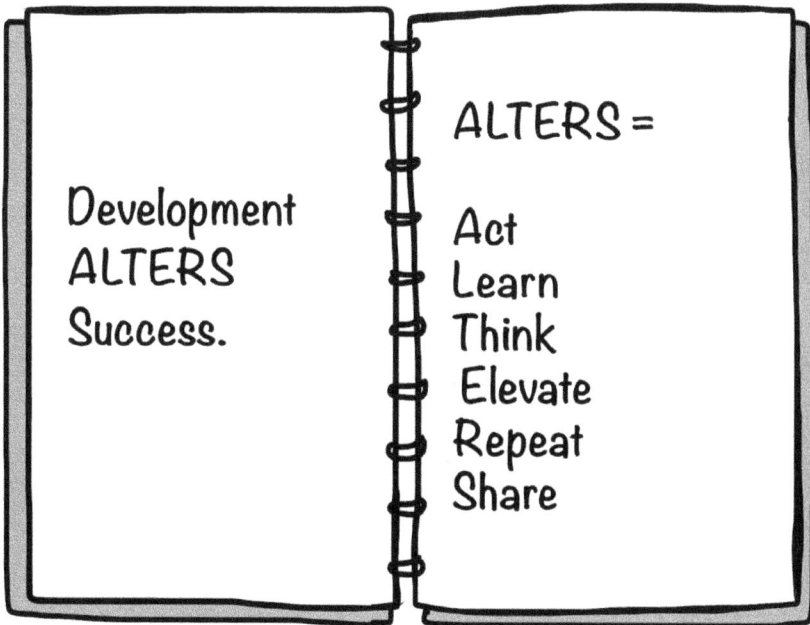

we act or do something, learn about the success we did or didn't achieve, think about what we can do differently to get a better result, elevate our game to do it differently, and then repeat the process. Finally, once we understand the journey that we've embarked upon, the final step is to share what we've learned with others.

"So you see, our group coaching meeting, and PIE itself, has nothing to do with baking. While your muffins are delicious, and your café certainly appears to be quite busy and you seem to have a winning recipe for your business, PIE offers a type of recipe to achieve greater personal success at work. I'm sure you could add value to our discussions and perhaps find value in the discussions taking place in our PIE group coaching sessions. If you have a few minutes for everyone to introduce themselves and tell you why they're here, then maybe you could join us for the morning. It would give you an opportunity to see if our sessions could help you discover a journey to greater success or to get better results more quickly. We will be discussing a simple method I discovered years ago and have been sharing ever since—that's where PIE comes in."

"I am intrigued, and I'll listen in if you don't mind," said the café owner curiously.

A young woman quickly stood. "Hi everyone, my name is Toni Keita," she stated. "I'm the VP of sales and marketing at a technology company and recently moved here from Canada to build an international presence. While I've had success in the past, I know there must be things I can do differently to achieve even more. That's why I'm here today."

Standing next to Toni was a confident looking, well-dressed man. "I'm Mathew Miller," he said boldly. "I'm visiting from California, where I work for a large finance corporation. After graduating from college, I quickly earned several promotions, but now I'm stuck. Everyone around me is advancing but I just can't seem to get another promotion. I figured it couldn't hurt to check this PIE thing out."

"I'm glad you're here, Toni and Mathew," said the PIE Guy. "How about you?" he asked, gesturing toward another man in the corner.

"My name is Charles Lee," the man stated with a charming smile. "I am the COO of a mountain bike manufacturer in Scotland. We're a mid-size company but want to expand our operations outside of the United Kingdom. I've got some big challenges ahead at work and need to get my head around what I need to do to make this a successful venture. I've heard good things about PIE, and not just the cherry variety."

After a good chuckle, the PIE Guy turned to the café owner again. "Why don't you tell us your name, a bit about your business, and your biggest business challenge? Then we can help you discover if the group is right for you."

Impressive amount of talent with interesting challenges. What do I have to lose? she thought. Then she said aloud, "My name is Clare Francis. I'm originally from England, but my family and I moved here to enjoy the abundant sunshine and outdoor adventures. I've always had a head for business and been good at baking, so I decided to start this café. I guess I've been pretty lucky so far. I wouldn't say I have any big business problems, though I suppose staff turnover could be

hurting us a bit. But I've always figured that if they don't want to be here, why should I encourage them to stay?"

"I'd definitely qualify staff turnover as a big business problem," said the PIE Guy. "Clare, as this group is meeting for the first time, why don't you join us for the morning? We're just off for a walk and talk. It's just a short walk and I'm going to share more about PIE as a development tool, it's origins, and the three lessons and two foundations for building greater success." He grabbed his sketchbook, stood, and turned toward the door, gesturing for the café owner and other group members to follow him. "Let's start walking while I tell you about a few people who have achieved greatness, often despite daunting obstacles."

Together they walked out the door and began strolling down the sidewalk under a brilliant blue, cloudless sky. The PIE Guy began. "There is a famous entrepreneur named Richard Branson. Maybe you've heard of him. Born in London in 1950, he started his first business venture at the age of 17. It was a magazine called *Student*, and despite his dyslexia and history of poor academic performance, it was an overnight success. Branson labored hard and branched out from publishing into record sales, opening a shop on Oxford Street in London staffed by other young people who were also new to business. This inspired the name Virgin, which eventually became Virgin Records, a highly successful record label. He later launched Virgin Atlantic Airways, Virgin Mobile, and Virgin Australia. At present, Sir Richard Charles Nicholas Branson is worth an estimated $4.9 billion in US dollars.

"But his is not the only tale of success I have to tell. There's Mark Zuckerberg, one of the founding fathers of Facebook, now one of the 100 wealthiest and most influential people in the world despite dropping out of Harvard.

"And J.K. Rowling, author of the Harry Potter fantasy series. Born in Gloucestershire in 1965, Rowling was initially employed as a researcher and secretary for Amnesty International when she conceived the idea for her first novel. Several family tragedies followed, but over the course of five years she managed to progress from living on welfare to becoming a multimillionaire.

"And Naveen Selvadurai. You may not have heard of him, but you've probably heard of Foursquare. That joint venture made him most of his money, but before that, he worked with well-known brands including Nokia, Sun Microsystems, and Sony.

"Catherine Cook is another great example. No stranger to the world of online social networking, she actually helped create that industry at the age of 18 when she co-launched MyYearBook.com, which is now MeetMe.com. Another self-made millionaire, Catherine has generated most of her success through mergers, acquisitions, and taking her company public.

"To be fair, the last two didn't have major challenges to overcome, they just accomplished amazing things." The PIE Guy paused for a moment to catch his breath. The group had reached the top of a very steep incline and everyone needed to cool down. Together they surveyed the landscape before them as the PIE Guy once again began to speak.

"Look at those glorious mountains," he exclaimed, gesturing toward the Rockies in the distance. "They remind me of another inspirational figure, Jamie Andrew. He's just a normal guy from Scotland, but his willpower is astounding. At the height of his climbing career, he was caught in a horrendous storm in the French Alps and was trapped on a ridge of ice for five days without anything more than basic emergency provisions for one night. While trapped on that ridge of ice, he lost his best friend and climbing partner, and severe frostbite and hypothermia led to the amputation of his hands and feet. But he didn't let that keep him down. No indeed. After his recovery, he continued to make amazing mountain ascents and achieve other incredible physical challenges across the globe

as a quadruple amputee, while raising thousands for charity and encouraging others to reach for their full potential.

"It's so fantastic to think about and see what individuals like these have done with their lives," said the PIE Guy, as the group turned away from their view of the mountain to join him on his trek down the other side of the hill. "But you don't have to be a great athlete, or famous, or have tremendous amounts of money to achieve great things. You just have to know how to do it. I'm here to help you discover exactly that."

As he fanned out his cape with another quick twirl, he continued, "I haven't always been a superhero working with people to transform their lives and dramatically improve their success. In fact, I've only been sporting this cape since the early 2000s. Before that, I had many of my own lessons to learn.

"Let me take you on a journey across time that includes brief stops in the military, Alaska's Aleutian Islands, and a university before a story or two from the corporate world. If this were a comic book, I suppose you could call it my origin story. However you want to label those years, one thing is certain: They taught me the importance of three lessons around Preparedness, Image, and Effort as well as two foundations for achieving greater success—the importance of people around me, and reviewing my plan for sustainable success. My first lesson, Lesson 1, was about Preparedness, and it all started with push-ups.

"Lesson 1 was learned during my military experience," said the PIE Guy. "Here's a short story to put it into context."

LESSON 1 - PREPAREDNESS

"Doing my utmost to excel in the military, I constantly found myself asking questions and learning what I needed to do to be successful. I soon discovered that this initial military environment was a game and if I were to win at the game, I needed to figure out the rules to the game. Part of the game was to understand the role of the training officers – they were preparing us for all elements of service: physical, mental and emotional. It was their role to ensure we had the tools necessary to perform as individuals and key members of a team.

"Much of the training in the beginning of my service was a combination of physical training, field exercises and classroom time studying to ensure we were ready for many different scenarios. It was a challenging process, but very rewarding as I discovered that I was learning how to prepare for even greater success – something I'd come to value my entire life.

"Preparedness was an enormous part of my military experience. We prepared for the physical demands of long days and nights in the field. We prepared for success by practicing our skills and building knowledge that would help us achieve greater success in whatever our task. It seemed as though we were always preparing. Whenever I felt as though I had mastered what they had wanted me to learn there was another twist to a scenario.

"I couldn't help constantly thinking scenarios through, looking at things from different angles - always looking for how the system could be improved. I wanted to improve processes and increase efficiencies, neither of which could be accomplished without asking questions.

What I learned quickly was that success in my role was to prepare myself based on what had been learned before my time and to align with other team members, explore options and deliver results. Here lay my first lesson in understanding the importance of being prepared as a key to success. Needless to say, the value I drew from my military service will always be part of my success, but now I help others with or without military experience prepare for success in their careers.

"Here's the link to PIE and my first lesson of three from P. I. & E. that came from my military experience," said the PIE Guy, pausing to display the next page in his sketchbook.

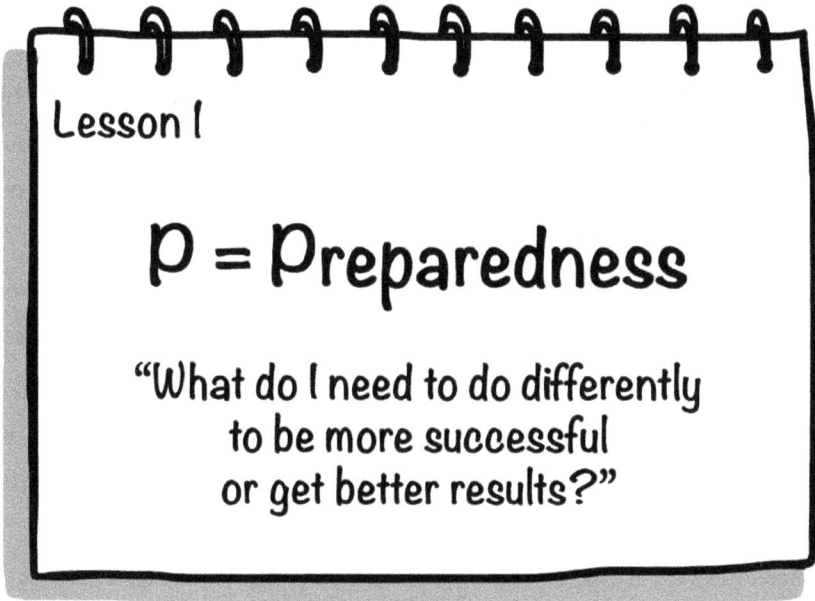

Lesson I

P = Preparedness

"What do I need to do differently to be more successful or get better results?"

"Preparedness is vital. Being prepared for success requires us to ask ourselves what we need to do differently to get better results. You guys and gals are already on the right track, as just being a part of this group demonstrates your desire to make changes—even if you don't yet know what you need to do differently."

LESSON 2 - IMAGE

"My second lesson in building greater success occurred after my military service and toward the end of my college education. It related to how I was perceived. This lesson, which I now call Image, is the 'I' in PIE. During my senior year, I took a semester off to earn money as a commercial crab fisherman in Alaska's Aleutian Islands. These crabs were huge with leg spans of 5 to 6 feet! These are some of the largest crabs in the world and were found in water about half a mile deep. If you are unfamiliar with that part of the world, 30-foot waves pick boats up and put them down—over and over again every 30 seconds. It's not a place you want to be if you have an issue with seasickness.

"Fortunately, seasickness wasn't my problem. My problem was the deck boss. He was a rather large guy who had spent many years fishing for crabs. He didn't say much—his style of communication would have worked well in the days when a series of grunts and chest bumps were enough to convey one's needs—but he was knowledgeable.

"He knew a thing or two about crab fishing, welding, and fixing broken parts on the boat, and he was, after all, the deck boss so people listened to him. It didn't hurt that he was 6'4" and weighed as much as a military tank. I, on the other hand, was the smallest guy on the boat at 5'10" and 180 pounds. He ruled the seas, or at least the boat, and as with others on the boat, he and I eventually had a disagreement.

"It didn't take me long to realize that his brawn wasn't superior to my brain. I needed to influence him quickly, so I created a particular image of myself by sharing a carefully selected story that convinced him to allow me to carry on with my job as the baiter without any contusions or additional confrontations. Ask me about the story later if you'd like. I'm happy to share this amusing tale of how I created a unique image or personal brand—it's part of the second lesson of PIE," the PIE Guy said as he turned another page in his sketchbook and presented it to the group.

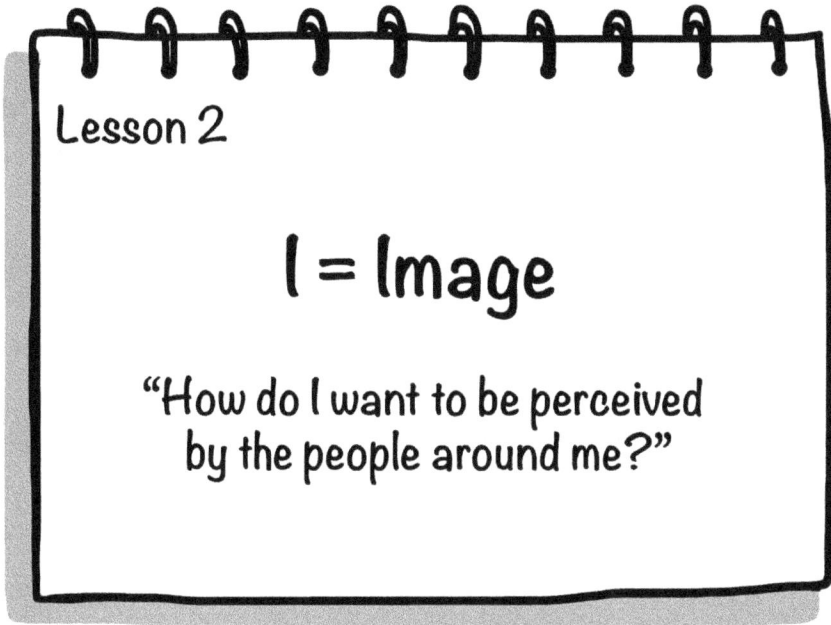

Lesson 2

I = Image

"How do I want to be perceived by the people around me?"

"How others perceive us is important in our ability to build success in our lives," he stated emphatically.

"These first two lessons are important but do not create success alone. As we look at the mountains before us, think back to the early explorers, indigenous people, and the settlers that first saw these giants looming from the horizon. The challenges they must have had to overcome to prosper in that wild mountainous environment is incredible. It reminds me of the third lesson I want to share with you."

LESSON 3 - EFFORT

"When I finally made it back to land, I returned to college to finish my undergraduate degree and to search for my first corporate role. It was during a grueling round of interviews that I learned my third lesson of PIE. Lesson 3 taught me the importance of energy, inertia, and engagement, which I now tie together into the word Effort. As you can imagine, Effort takes many forms from physical to cerebral. Let me try and bring Effort to life to highlight its importance. After going through several rounds of local interviews, I was short-listed and ended up traveling across the country for my final round of interviews. I found myself standing in front of a senior vice president at my company of choice. He had his feet up on the desk, and as he leaned back in his big leather chair, at what was to be my final meeting with this company, he said to me, 'I'm sorry, I just don't see a fit here.'

"My mind went into hyperdrive. I wanted to work for his company and I thought they wanted me. After all, I had passed a series of local interviews in Colorado before they flew me to the East Coast for the remainder of the selection process. That alone indicated I was one of their top candidates.

"I quickly looked around, thinking about all the research I had done prior to traveling to their corporate office for this final round of interviews. Noting the photographs and memorabilia, I remembered from my research that this senior vice president was a bit of a baseball star during his college days. Smiling confidently, I suggested that they take a look at improving their recruitment process—as they had spent a tremendous amount of money on a candidate who wasn't the right fit—before I turned the subject to baseball. We laughed and joked for 45 minutes before he offered me the job. Effort this time was my investment in researching the company and the people I would be meeting throughout the interview process, ensuring I had the best possible opportunity to know and understand them and to explore the possibility of building a mutually beneficial relationship.

"This taught me the third lesson of PIE: What form of and how much Effort is needed," he said, once again presenting the group with a page in the sketchbook.

Lesson 3

E = Effort

"What form should my effort take and how much is required?"

"Effort takes many forms, and this time my effort was in using my brain and linking what I had researched with my observations to build success. In other situations, it could be carving time out of a busy calendar to schedule personal development, sitting down to write a vision statement, or talking to an employee about their career path," he said, closing the sketchbook as the group rounded the corner and approached a shady expanse of grass. "Let's rest here for a bit."

Everyone made themselves comfortable under the expansive branches of a large cottonwood tree and waited for the PIE Guy to continue with his story.

"Although I eventually found more success in the corporate sector than I did in the military, my inability to be as successful as I wanted to be perplexed me. I was applying Preparedness, Image, and Effort in my everyday life, but I still wasn't progressing as fast as I wanted. It was shortly after starting my corporate career that I finally realized that I was missing two additional key components to success. These additional components are different from the three lessons of PIE that I've shared with you and so I call them the two 'foundations of success.' While PIE is about what each of us needs to do slightly differently to achieve better results, the foundations are how we build our PIE.

"Just to manage your brain capacity and energy levels, there are two stories I'd like to share with you that will help bring the foundations to life. By the way, I believe storytelling is one of the most powerful methods of learning. Storytelling allows us to more readily transfer theory into our own lives in a more practical way. So, here's another real example I'd like to share with you that demonstrates the value of the 1st Foundation of PIE.

1ˢᵗ FOUNDATION OF PIE – SUCCESS REQUIRES A VILLAGE

"One day Dave, a senior executive in the company I was working for, invited me to join a process improvement team. The number of people packed into the conference room for the first meeting shocked me.

"Sitting around the table was a fantastic amount of investment if you calculated the hourly wages of the senior vice presidents, and the heads of marketing, operations, finance, and the distribution center attending the meeting. I figured the president of the company must have sanctioned all of this and it must have been something very critical to the business. I was right if you consider changing a warehouse packing label to be critical to the business. To me, it seemed a tremendous waste of time and money.

"Within five minutes of the start of this meeting, I had sketched out a solution to the problem and given it to Dave. But to my surprise, he didn't stop the meeting to share my suggestion with everyone. Instead, as the discussions progressed, each department shared the impact of this ill-designed packing label. The cost to the organization—due to errors, returns, and lost products—was actually staggering. I was astounded.

"In the end, my initial suggestion turned out to be the chosen solution. However, I had to question myself: Had I just been lucky, or would I be able to replicate my results, proving to everyone that

I was good at my job? Maybe there was something else to learn from this experience above and beyond the immediate experience—something that I could apply to future opportunities to catapult my success to where I knew it could be. The lesson gained clarity in my head as I thought about the experience. This was a team of people working on a common issue—not pointing the finger of accusation at one another, but instead collaborating with one another to find a workable solution.

"After thinking about this experience for a few weeks, I began to see the importance of something even greater than teams collaborating to achieve a result. I began to see how people worked collaboratively together to achieve success. I was fascinated by how people who weren't necessarily a team in structure still cared about outcomes and were aligned to something greater than themselves. I explored the depths of my experiences, thinking about great leaders I have been fortunate enough to work for and others I have observed at close proximity—leaders who have achieved success by surrounding themselves with people who collaboratively help build greater success. It wasn't always a team, and it's more than a network. Success required something more. This lead me to the 1st Foundation of PIE, which highlights the importance and value others play in building greater personal success. People can help us, and we can help people achieve better results. This first foundation is fundamental to building success. Our success is limited if we try to achieve success on our own."

The PIE Guy showed his audience the next page in the sketchbook.

1st Foundation of PIE

Success Requires a Village

"Collaborating with others ensures success is achieved faster and is more sustainable. I believe our success is linked to the people that surround us. I call this our village. Members of our village are those with whom we share a vested interest. I have been fortunate to meet and work with a wide variety of people who have shared their wisdom and experience with me. These were friends from college and people I had met through the workplace, such as Robin, Hilary, Wick, Grant, McCool—yes, that was his real name—and Kathy. Although I'll leave their stories out for the sake of time, they taught me the value of planning, challenging myself, empowerment, and the power of positive self-conversations. They also shared readings with me by some of the great motivational and development gurus and theorists, such as Anthony Robbins, Ken Blanchard, and Stephen Covey. They were also open to sharing specific feedback about how I could change to ensure greater success. These people made up my early village. Some have left and new people have joined, but one thing is certain: My villagers are there for me, and when called upon, I am there for them."

2ⁿᵈ FOUNDATION OF PIE – SUCCESS REQUIRES PROGRESS REVIEWS

"The last story I have to share with you introduces what I believe is the 2ⁿᵈ Foundation of PIE. While studying for my master's degree, Professor Colin Beard introduced me to Dr. Roger Greenaway's work on reviewing. The premise behind Dr. Greenaway's research is that it's an active cyclical process to enable people of all abilities to use their experiences as a major source of learning and development. This reflective process enables and empowers people to review their experiences and to develop the awareness that is critical to becoming better learners and effectively increase their ability to sustainably get better results. Reviewing where we are against where we want to be allows us to correct the course we are on and to get back on track to achieving greater success.

"I am a firm believer in reviewing. It's especially important in the ever-changing environment of business. 'What am I doing well?' and 'What could I be doing slightly better?' are two questions you'll find me using continuously in my work. I've even used them successfully with my children as well as with myself, as I am continually trying to become a better father, husband, coach, and leader. The power in reviewing is incredible. It helps us to understand what is and isn't working, and keeps us on track to achieve greater success. If we think about success as a journey we are embarking on, where there are multiple paths to success, every once in awhile we need to correct the direction we are traveling to ensure we reach the points along the path that are important to us. This is what reviewing allows us to do—course correct when necessary. We'll be unpacking this concept, and looking at a review tool I use to simplify and make reviewing

2nd Foundation of PIE

Success Requires Progress Reviews

easier and more relevant, toward the end of our time together.

"After completing my master's degree in 2002, I revisited the three key lessons of Preparedness, Image, and Effort and the two foundations of PIE: success requires a village and progress reviews, numerous times, sharing them with others to help shorten their path to greater success. Since then, when working as the PIE Guy with small companies or global organizations, teams or individuals, my message has been the same—it's about combining these five components to help you be more effective in your role. I soon discovered that the key to building success falls into a pattern. Most importantly, that pattern is replicable, and the pattern requires more than being prepared, creating the right image, and putting in the effort. Building success requires an aligned village of people to support you and a process of continually reviewing what you do."

As they all stood and prepared to stroll back to where they started, the café owner, Clare, said, "Let me see if I have this straight. PIE isn't a secret. We don't have to be wealthy, genius thinkers, or out-of-the-box innovators to use it. Anyone, from a café owner to an entrepreneur, or a manager to a COO, can benefit from the lessons and foundations of PIE."

"That's correct for me and for the others I have worked with," the PIE Guy agreed. "As far as the famous people I mentioned, it's easy to find the same elements incorporated in their success, even though I had nothing to do with it. What I've done is to build a simple model based on what I've experienced, witnessed, and read about, and I happen to call it PIE.

"Let's head back to the café and continue our discussion. I have a few things to share that require a flipchart."

The PIE Guy continued his discourse on their way back to the café saying, "Standing for Preparedness, Image, and Effort, PIE is a personal development tool everyone can use to achieve their goals, drive change, and build success. Even better, PIE allows you to do this quickly and effectively with the minimum amount of disruption to your daily activities." The PIE Guy opened the door of Café Creo Prosperitas, and entering, he gestured to the rest of the group to follow him to the corner table containing their belongings.

Charles, the COO, interjected, "That's what's needed—something simple that works. I've been to many workshops that deliver learning that makes sense when in the isolation of the workshop, but as soon as I am back at work, it seems too complex or too time consuming to implement." He quickly adjusted his eyeglasses and then said, "Whenever I've made a big push to move forward in my career in the past, I've had to devote most of my time to the process. Unfortunately, this has been to the detriment of other things in my life. I don't have time for that right now, nor am I willing to gamble with the other areas of my life again."

"I understand, Charles. Many people experience this, and it's why I advocate continual progress when building greater success, even if those steps toward success may be small steps," the PIE Guy replied. "I've spent numerous years helping both organizations and employees implement change to improve efficiency, achieve better results, and increase productivity. There are a few success-related questions that I have been asked over and over again."

The Pie Guy paused at the flipchart to reveal the following:

Typical Comments

- I want to sustain my career trajectory and could use some ideas.

- I want to be a great leader but don't know how.

- I do great work, but no one recognizes my contributions.

- Some people are just luckier in business than others.

"Keep in mind, the majority of people who've made these comments are confident, knowledgeable, and driven," said the PIE Guy. "Early on in my career, I was also scratching my head in bewilderment, wondering why these people weren't experiencing the kind of success their character seemed to deserve. It was only after thinking about my own lessons, and drawing parallels between them and the people asking these questions, did I begin to realize the power of the three recurring lessons—Preparedness, Image, and Effort—and the two foundations for building greater success—Our Village and Reviewing Progress. These lessons were consistent across the different populations I was working with, across cultures and national boundaries, and from leaders to teams to individual employees. These people were thinking about personal change, which is the precursor to effective and lasting organizational change.

"Now that I understand the basis of these three lessons and the foundations of success, I try to guide the people I work with to a new series of questions specifically linked to building success." The PIE Guy turned the page on his flipchart.

Toni, the VP of a sales and marketing department from Canada, said, "These questions seem organized and more logical. They are questions I need answers to. Any suggestions on next steps?"

"It's pretty simple," said the PIE Guy. "You need to take a look at the big picture, a task I can help you tackle. But embarking on this journey of self-improvement requires a willingness to change. And that willingness requires motivation, dedication, and an ability to realize that improvement is possible."

1. Where do I find my criteria for success?

2. How do I discover my image perception difference?

3. What do I need to do to achieve more success in my role?

4. Who can help me achieve this success?

5. How can I sustain creating success in my career?

Mathew, the financial guy from California chimed in. "I've been to a lot of workshops," he said as he leveled a doubtful look at the group as a whole, "and personal change is hard. It takes a lot of work and time to make those changes."

"Yes it does, but it shouldn't get in the way of your day job," responded the PIE Guy. "Small steps are all you really need to take in order to make progress. I can help you create something I like to call a <u>Success PIE.</u> It helps people to achieve greater success by identifying what you need to do differently to get better results. It's important to be realistic in what you are trying to accomplish within a reasonable amount of time. Your Success PIE combines your dreams, thoughts, and direction into a series of development activities to help you realize your goals."

The PIE Guy motioned to the chairs and said, "If you'd all take a seat for a moment, I'd like to provide a quick recap of what we've covered today. I bet you I can do it in three sentences or less."

The group sat and waited expectantly for him to continue. Several people removed notebooks and pens from their briefcases.

"Anyone and everyone—from the baristas in this café to its owner, and entry-level employees to CEOs—can achieve greater success even in the face of incredible obstacles if they learn to use the lesson of PIE and its foundations. PIE is a personal development tool that stands for Preparedness, Image, and Effort. It will help you analyze your personal situation, develop a series of actions to make sustainable improvements, and learn from and work with your village while reviewing and course correcting.

"That was three sentences!" he concluded with a laugh. "And that's all I have to say about PIE today. But I would encourage all of you to take a minute or two to write down anything that resonates with you from our walk-and-talk discussion. Look for connections within your real-life situation, and think about what you'd like to get out of our next session."

Clare said, "I really want to know more about the ingredients in your PIE. I feel like I've had just a taste today and I think I need an entire slice."

"And you shall have one," the PIE Guy laughed once more. "Why don't we all meet here again tomorrow, and I'll talk more about the ingredients you'll need to create your own personal Success PIE."

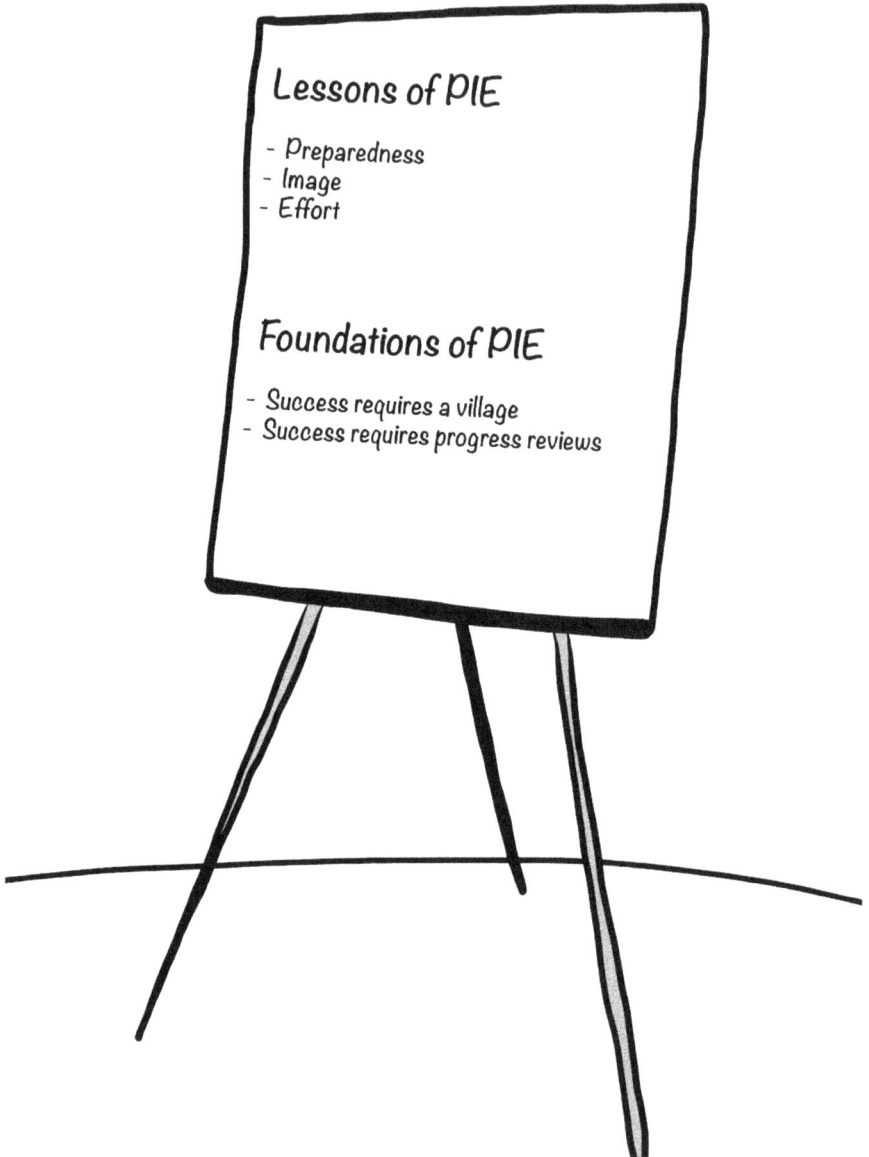

Lessons of PIE

- Preparedness
- Image
- Effort

Foundations of PIE

- Success requires a village
- Success requires progress reviews

CHAPTER 1

INGREDIENTS FOR YOUR SUCCESS PIE

"Regardless of who you are or
what you have been, you can be
what you want to be."

W. Clement Stone

As the sun began to peek over the eastern horizon, Clare unlocked the door to Café Creo Prosperitas. She had coffee to make and muffins to bake before 5:00 a.m. when the café would officially open for the day's business. She deposited her purse and coat in her office, put on her apron, and got directly to work. An hour later, her employees began to file in.

"Rebecca," Clare said to one of them, a young woman who had quickly become her most reliable barista, "I'd like you to take over as manager for the day."

"Sure," Rebecca replied. "I'd be happy to. I hope everything is okay with you."

"I'm fine," said Clare. "There's going to be a group meeting about professional development here today and I want to participate without worrying about everything that needs to be done behind the counter."

She returned to the office to take off her apron as a line of customers began to form. Among them were the professionals from the previous day's walk-and-talk. Once they had their coffee and muffins, they situated themselves in the back corner of the café and began to chat about their experience.

"I don't know about you," said Toni, "but I'm looking forward to today's meeting. My mind was racing and I could barely fall asleep last night because I was thinking about the famous people we talked about yesterday and realized that, just like the PIE Guy said, they had to take small steps to make it to where they are now. I'm looking forward to learning more so I can start applying this to my career."

"I slept just fine," said Mathew. "While I appreciate that PIE is something we can all supposedly use, I'm not convinced it's the answer. There are so many theories out there. What's to say that this one is really going to make a difference in my life?"

At that moment, the PIE Guy arrived in all his colorful glory. "Good morning!" he exclaimed cheerfully, "I see we have a new face with us today. Welcome Stuart, nice to put a face to the voice on the other end of the telephone. While I go grab some coffee, why don't the rest of you introduce yourselves?"

Clare, Toni, Mathew, and Charles introduced themselves to the new member of the group. Then the newcomer explained why he had decided to join.

"I'm Stuart Williams," he said with a winning grin and an Australian accent. "I work for a large national retailer. I was promoted to a regional manager because I was a cracking-good store department manager. My company put me on their "Fast Track Management Development" program, which means I am involved in lots of training and have access to external support as well. Our HR business partner suggested I look at the PIE Guy and see if his methods of personal development would work for me. I heard that his Success PIE was a simple tool, which I like. My days are crammed with meetings and I don't want to spend days and weeks learning some complicated development tool that will be hard to implement."

"I feel the same way," Mathew interjected. "I was just talking about how many people are selling similar concepts these days—and they all claim to do the same thing."

"I completely understand your concerns, Stuart and Mathew," said the PIE Guy, who had returned with his coffee and muffin. "I am a firm believer that 'simple works'—it's actually one of my mantras. One of the most important things to consider about your personal development is which method interests you and fits with your lifestyle and work. Then it's far easier to make a commitment to learn, find time in busy schedules, and put it into practice.

"It's also important to know why you are interested in learning and developing, and what it will achieve," continued the PIE Guy. "Once we are aware of these things, it's about making simple decisions. Simple decisions include how you chose to attend this meeting today. This is a simple decision that could have tremendous positive implications on what you are able to achieve. When we break down our complex lives into simple decisions, we begin to make real progress, and we aren't able to hide behind the complexities of our work and lives. Let's get cracking on today's conversations.

Your success is linked to the choices you make.

"So a hearty welcome, Stuart, and welcome back Clare, Toni, Mathew, and Charles. I'm thrilled that all of you have chosen to join me today to learn more about the ingredients required to whip up your own personal Success PIE."

The PIE Guy continued, "An important part of understanding your success ingredients is to understand more about what drives you to work, learn, and earn. Once you discover those drivers, the other elements we'll discuss later on will become easier to fit into place. Let's start by identifying what you do, what you enjoy about what you do, what you find challenging, and what barriers to success are standing in your way to achieving something greater."

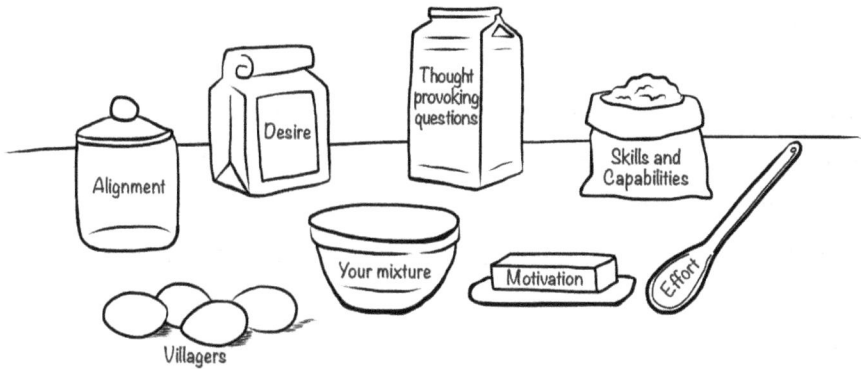

The PIE Guy turned to the café owner. "Clare, why don't you tell us a bit about what you have to do each morning before your first customer arrives. Be specific, if you please."

"Well," said Clare, "I usually arrive two hours before the café opens. I grind the coffee, start the roaster, mix up four batches of muffins, and get them into the oven. Then I restock the product shelves and make sure the baristas will have everything they need behind the counter when the first customers arrive. It's fast-paced and sometimes a bit stressful."

"Sounds busy as you prepare each morning," the PIE Guy noted. "What would happen if you didn't show up here to do what needs to be done to prepare for the day?"

"My customers wouldn't have any coffee or muffins," Clare replied. "My café wouldn't make any money and I wouldn't be able to pay my mortgage. I'd end up on the street in a cardboard box, begging for change," Clare concluded with a smirk.

"Yikes," said the PIE Guy smiling. "And when you're baking the muffins, what are you looking for?"

"Good muffins are a generous size," Clare said. "They are golden brown on top, full of plump fruit or gooey chocolate chips, and have a nice, slightly moist texture. And they smell delicious.

"But I'm pretty sure it's not just the muffins that make my café so popular with local customers—even though they are the best in the area. It's also not just the fact that we brew only the most fragrant, delicious, and ethically-sourced coffee, either," she continued. "I've taken great pains to create a welcoming atmosphere. From the not-too-bright lighting to the cheerfully painted walls, and from the comfortable chairs to the authentic friendliness of my staff, everything about my café is designed to relax and satisfy."

"Fascinating," said the PIE Guy. "So what I'm hearing is your success is also based on your image, in addition to running many aspects of your café not just as well as, but better than your competitors."

"Yes, that sounds correct," responded Clare.

"But let me ask you another question," said the PIE Guy. "If you weren't in this town, nestled against a backdrop of mountains where people have multiple coffee shops from which to choose, but were instead in a small town with no competition, would you still invest so much time and energy?"

"Maybe not," Clare said thoughtfully. "But I would still want to give my customers a quality experience."

"Of course, and you've determined what you need to do in order to achieve that. So you'd match your effort with what you want your customers to experience. Here's another question: Why do you do what you do? What motivated you to choose to open and run a café?" the PIE Guy prodded.

"Well, I always dreamed of owning a business," said Clare. "And it was important to me to not just start one, but to run it using a business model that could also provide a good living for the people who work for me."

"But you could do that in many different industries," the PIE Guy stated. "What in particular made you choose to build a business in hospitality? Why a café?"

Clare reflected for a few seconds and then said, "I think it has something to do with giving people a place to come where they can have great conversations. I used to do that in my own living room at home before opening the café. I wanted to recreate that environment here, only better."

"Now we're getting somewhere!" said the PIE Guy with his usual enthusiasm. "By answering my simple questions around what you do, why you do it, and who does it better, we have identified how Preparedness, Image, and Effort are all critical in the success of your café. Now we're getting closer to your specific success ingredients."

He continued, "Your success ingredients are the things that make you slightly different from other café owners, and they are the reason why visitors come back to your café again and again. This special blend of ingredients is unique to your situation and will become the basis for further conversations around PIE and the next steps you will take.

"To recap," the PIE Guy said, flipping to a page in his trusty sketchbook, "where your success ingredients come from depends on the following…"

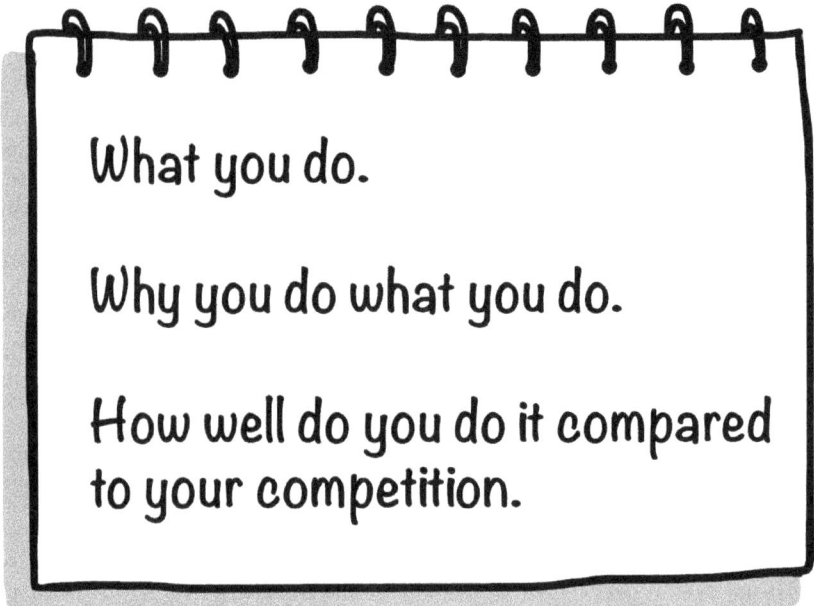

What you do.

Why you do what you do.

How well do you do it compared to your competition.

He gestured to each line as he continued, "You can be the CEO of a large corporation or a window washer at a hotel and still benefit from identifying the unique ingredients in your Success PIE."

"If you like a good metaphor, here's an example. Let's say you've been fortunate enough to spend a good deal of time traveling outside your home country. You love bread, so you've made a hobby of tasting the breads from every country you visit on your travels. You quickly realize that just because breads share common ingredients— yeast, flour, and water to be specific—they still vary greatly in their taste, consistency, and aroma. A croissant from a bakery in France tastes nothing like an American baker's attempt to replicate it—no offense, Clare.

"You can be a successful analyst in a boutique consultancy or a senior manager in a global corporate business, but your success ingredients are going to be slightly different depending on you and on the country and company in which you work. This is why there's no magic pill or magic wand that can tell you your specific ingredients for success—but there are resources at your disposal that can help you identify them. Feedback from you line manager or your role profile, some people call it a job description, provide good starting points in identifying some of the ingredients to increase your success at work."

The PIE Guy turned to Stuart. "What's your take on all of this so far, Stuart? Do you think PIE is something you can benefit from in your career?" he asked.

"I certainly hope so!" Stuart replied enthusiastically. "Like Clare, my work involves providing the public with things they need or want.

But instead of baking muffins and brewing coffee, I'm providing them with information to help them make informed purchases about products for projects they are working on at home."

"This is good," said the PIE Guy, nodding his head in encouragement. "More details, please."

"I want to make sure my customers continue to choose our stores for their purchases. I have to ensure all their questions get answered, and help them with product suggestions that could make their projects easier to complete," Stuart continued. "I also have to ensure each store in my region keeps their store clean, controls shrinkage, and maintains the company culture."

"I see a few similarities between your and Clare's roles, although the scale of your operations, Stuart, may bring more complexity," said the PIE Guy.

"It think so as well, and that's partially why I'm here. It can be overwhelming when I think about the complete list of what I have to do, from hiring, managing, and motivating a team to increasing sales, overseeing the buying process, and maximizing profits, all the while making sure the customers feel like they've been treated with respect, and ensuring our company culture is consistent across a big area where many local cultures exist and differ greatly. It's the biggest role I've ever had, and I'm exhausted." Stuart concluded by saying, "So, if you can help me with this, perhaps I won't be as exhausted and I'll feel like my last promotion was worth it!"

"That was quite a list!" the PIE Guy said. "This is what building greater success is all about, and this is the type of conversation we need to have at the beginning of our time together. It's important to have real conversations that matter instead of talking niceties, and I am glad we've jumped right into the important stuff. We need to identify the things in our work that we have to do and then dig a bit deeper by looking at why we do what we do, as well as what we want to do slightly differently to get better results. You've rattled off a long list of things required for success. Do you need help in all of the areas or is there something specific?"

> # In order to prioritize your development create time in your schedule.

Stuart responded, "It's like you've been speaking to my line manager! There are a few specific things I need to do better, but in order to do it better, I need more time in the day!"

The PIE Guy replied, "Perhaps, the larger issue is around leadership or time management. You said you were recently promoted and that you are in your company's 'Talent' program.

Clearly you have been good at your job in the past and your company has rewarded you for it," recalled the PIE Guy.

"That's correct, but sometimes I feel they just wanted to throw someone else's work/life balance off kilter." Stuart continued, "I know that's not true, but it feels like it. I'm hoping to explore what is within my power to make a difference."

"Well," said the PIE Guy, "that's what we're here for, Stuart, and we will be diving deeper into this as the week continues. The next question I'm curious about is why do you do what you do?"

"It's pretty simple," Stuart responded. "I love my work and working with customers. It doesn't actually feel like work, although the hours can be long, which can be draining at times. Since receiving my promotion, the hours have gotten even longer and the pressure has increased. Although I truly do still enjoy my work, my fiancée says that I was more enjoyable to be around *before* my promotion. So now, I'm beginning to question if this company is right for me."

The PIE Guy nodded with understanding. "Thank you for sharing this with us. I want to reassure you and let you know that we all go through changes similar to this. In a few days' time we will be talking more about change to help understand the expectations we place upon ourselves. We'll revisit this throughout the week as we start taking a closer look at the individual components of PIE."

"Mathew," he said, noticing that the well-dressed professional was leaning forward as if wanting to speak. "Would you like to share what you think your Success PIE ingredients might be?"

"Sure," Mathew boldly replied. "I'm not the CEO of the company, so I don't really have to worry about the competitors of our global financial service organization. I just want to do my job well and be recognized for it—such as with a promotion. That would make me feel successful."

The PIE Guy wanted to hear more. "Go on and elaborate a bit more, if you wouldn't mind."

Mathew cleared his throat and began. "Our human resource business partner held a workshop on this a year ago. Let me see if I can recall the main points. To figure out what we need to do to perform our job well, we can look at the role description for our position and ask line managers for feedback," said Mathew. "The job description tells me what I need to accomplish in my job. And the feedback tells me what I am doing well and what I could be doing better."

"Nicely remembered," exclaimed the PIE Guy. "Is there anything else?"

"When possible, I should try to do more than just what is in my role description," Mathew responded. "If my workload allows, I should try to take on additional duties to help out others and my bosses. That way, my bosses can achieve more in their job. To me, this sounds like bosses are trying to get us to do their work."

The PIE Guy said, "Just like most things, Mathew, there are multiple positions we can take throughout life, a line of thinking that falls on the more cynical side or a line of thinking where we assume positive intent. By adopting the former, does it get you any closer to your promotion? Conversely, by adopting the latter, you could think through what your human resource business partner may be trying to instill, which sounds like career progression for those interested. Your recall on the workshop you attended was spot on, Mathew. May I ask you a question?"

"Sure," Mathew replied.

"How much have you implemented from that workshop?"

"Not a thing. I didn't need to. I get great results, and always have. My bonus is always at the max," said Mathew with pride.

"Congratulations. Perhaps by the end of the week, some light will be shed on your particular situation to help you discover something you can do differently to get a better result, such as that promotion you mentioned," the PIE Guy remarked.

"I look forward to that part," Mathew mused. "There is one thing I'm not very clear on. You asked why I do what I do. There are lots of reasons, I suppose, from taking care of my family to paying the mortgage and car payments to being able to afford a nice vacation."

"Yes, that's why you *need* money," responded the PIE Guy. "But *why* do you go to work? What gets you out of bed in the morning?"

"My alarm," Mathew said with a laugh, and then paused to think. "You know what? I actually *enjoy* going to the office and getting on with my work. It also allows me to earn a decent living. I want to make sure that my kids don't have to deal with the barriers that I had to deal with growing up.

"My father never earned a lot of money, and my mother stayed at home to take care of all of us. We couldn't afford after-school activities that carried fees. That meant I couldn't be on the football team or other school teams, even though I was good enough to play many sports. If I had been allowed to play, I would have been able to go to college on a scholarship rather than making student loan payments for 20 years.

"I want my kids to be able to do everything they dream of doing," Mathew concluded. "That's why I work."

"That's a wonderful reason," said the PIE Guy. Turning to Toni, he asked, "Has any of this helped you to start defining your ingredients for success?"

"Actually, yes!" she responded excitedly. "In order to be successful in penetrating this new market, I have to help potential clients understand how we fill a niche in the market. I'm certainly working on that, and I'll be able to provide jobs for a number of professionals as a result. My reward is that I don't have to worry about finances — for the company or for myself. Oh yes, and winning! I love to beat the competition!"

The PIE Guy asked, "So how do you determine what you need to do to maintain that success once the competition starts to penetrate your niche market?"

"Well, my situation is a bit like Clare's," Toni said. "I need to be aware of what my competition is doing, know what my customers expect, and then do it all better."

"Yes!" the PIE Guy exclaimed. "You've hit upon an important topic close to my heart, 'Do it better,' or as I suggest, 'What can you do differently to get a better result?' We'll discuss that more in the near future. Why do you do what you do, Toni?"

"I haven't thought much about why I do what I do," said Toni. "I'm not a greedy person. I don't want people to lose their jobs or make other companies go out of business. But I do want a piece of the pie."

"Okay, thanks Toni, and how about you, Charles?" the PIE Guy asked.

What can you do slightly differently to get a better result?

"The conversation today has been interesting," Charles replied. "I can see how by identifying and focusing on the ingredients for success for the business, allows us to achieve impressive sales and significant growth in the racing products arena. But what I hadn't spent time thinking about before today are the ingredients necessary for my own personal success. I may need to talk to a few people before I can answer this question fully."

"Who do you intend to talk to?" asked the PIE Guy.

"I think I'd like to get the views of my family, the company's board of directors, my direct reports, and my personal assistant," said Charles.

"Excellent. You've hit on one of the two foundations that are so critical to success that we talked about yesterday, the village," said the PIE Guy. We've got a few things to talk about before we

The people you are reaching out to are called your "village". They will be instrumental in helping you build greater success.
I want help from all those people I've mentioned.
PIE

jump into the village, but it sounds like this is a natural part of your everyday thinking."

Charles asked, "So it's okay to involve others in the process of finding your ingredients for personal success?"

"It's not just okay," the PIE Guy responded, "it is essential. This is especially true as we move through stages of our lives. Our ingredients for success may change along with our career or family situation."

The PIE Guy looked at his watch and then stood. "Let's meet here again tomorrow," he said to the group. "I'm thinking we should get here early to experience Clare's opening procedures. We should be able to gain some valuable insight while helping Clare prepare for another successful day."

The group nodded their heads in agreement.

"One more thing," the PIE Guy said as they all began to gather their belongings. "I want you to remember that there is no magic pill you can take to create success. Some of the most important things in life require thinking time, time where you stop everything else and think about why you do what you do, and more importantly, what you could do slightly differently to get a better result."

Clare added, "It seems like the first step is to commit to our own development and really take ownership of our success and our future."

"I couldn't have said it more succinctly, Clare," the PIE Guy agreed.

He continued, "In the beginning of today's session, we discussed how in order to understand your success ingredients, you must first understand more about what drives you to work and earn. Once you discover those drivers, the other elements will become easier to fit into place. By taking the time to have these conversations, hopefully you have been exposed to many different ideas above and beyond your own thoughts. Take a moment to jot down things that have resonated from today's session. I look forward to seeing you all again tomorrow."

CHAPTER 2

P = PREPAREDNESS

"By failing to prepare, you are preparing to fail."

Benjamin Franklin

In the predawn hours of what local weathermen predicted was to be a gloriously sunny summer day, the PIE Guy's professional development group began to assemble outside the door of Café Creo Prosperitas. Toni was the first to arrive, just as eager as she was the previous day, to learn more about using PIE to take her already successful Canadian tech company to the next level in the American market.

Within minutes she was joined by Charles, the bicycle manufacturing company COO, who arrived, quite fittingly, on a beautifully designed, custom-built, black and red carbon-fiber mountain bike. As he was removing his helmet and gloves, Mathew pulled up in a silver 3-Series Mercedes. Before the well-mannered financial professional could cross the parking lot to join the others, the morning's peaceful birdcalls were interrupted by the whirring of helicopter blades and the ear-splitting, "Good day! Let's prepare for greater success!" shouted by the man rappelling from its cockpit.

It was the PIE Guy, only this time he wore a green camo army uniform under his colorful red and gold cape. Dropping lightly to the ground as he unhooked the rappelling line from his belt, he jogged to the café door.

"What a fabulous morning!" he exclaimed, enthusiastically shaking hands with Toni, Charles, and Mathew before knocking loudly on the door. "Let's get Clare's attention and get this session started!"

Within moments, Clare appeared, opened the door, and gestured for them to come inside, and stated, "Stuart rang and said that he won't be able to make it to today's session." The PIE Guy acknowledged her comment, but didn't miss a step. Once they had deposited their belongings at their usual table, they gathered near the counter.

The PIE Guy began, "You're probably wondering why I'm dressed like a soldier today. The answer is simple: Today we're going to talk more about Preparedness, a good military readiness term. While soldiers might have to be prepared to deploy for a mission, as business professionals you need to be prepared to embrace opportunity. Preparedness is a term used quite widely, and FEMA, the United States' Federal Emergency Management Agency, uses Preparedness in it's mission and goal to ensure the nation is ready for disasters, essentially setting the country up for success in scenarios that are less than welcoming. Well, when we talk about Preparedness, we are looking at two things: Setting ourselves up for success in periods of change, and understanding what we can do differently to get better results.

"Think about it for a moment. If someone presented you with an opportunity—let's say a promotion, Mathew, or a new account, Toni—and you needed to compete for it, how ready would you be to ensure success? In order to prepare for success, you have to understand why you want something and how it aligns with your goals. You also need to be familiar with your core competencies, what makes you unique and what you may need to do slightly differently to succeed. Understanding how all of those factors link to the people around your career and company will help you prepare for the future while being more successful in the present.

"If you're like many of the professionals I work with, you're probably thinking, *I'm prepared!* Believe me, I understand the desire to state that you are prepared. However, when you're dealing with the day-to-day demands of your job, it's all too easy to set preparation

Preparing for Greater
Success Requires:
- Self analysis
- 360 feedback
- Knowing what good looks like
- Support from my village
- Motivation
- A road map
- Development priorities
-
-
-

for the future aside in favor of the urgent here and now. Fortunately, creating your Success PIE will help you quickly paint a picture that illustrates *where* you need to focus your preparation energy in order to realize greater success.

"You must prepare both mentally and physically. Of course, mental preparation is the first step. If you don't understand the roadblocks and obstacles you face, you'll never be able to surmount them."

Noticing that Clare seemed particularly agitated, the PIE Guy paused for a moment. "I feel like we've put you under some additional pressure today, Clare," he said. "I hope our presence here isn't making your morning more stressful."

"No, I'm normally this stressed at the beginning of each day," Clare replied, going behind the counter to continue the day's preparations.

"I'm so sorry," said the PIE Guy. "I imagine those feelings aren't very enjoyable."

"It's okay," Clare said, gathering ingredients for the shop's popular muffins. "I know that by 7:00 a.m. all will be well. It's only the first two hours of my day that aren't that enjoyable, to say the least. After that, I can watch customers enjoy their experience…" Clare's words trailed off as she rummaged in a cupboard.

"Oh blimey!" she exclaimed, exasperated. "I'm almost out of chocolate chips!"

The PIE Guy calmly joined her behind the counter. "What would happen if you didn't have them?"

"We always have them," Clare stated. "They are the main ingredient in our signature muffin."

"I see," said the PIE Guy. "Let's think about those chocolate chips. What can you do to ensure that you never run out?"

"Actually, I could buy more of them at a time," said Clare. "But I don't have enough storage space for bigger bags."

"Anything else?" the PIE Guy prodded.

"I guess I could make fewer chocolate chip muffins," Clare replied.

"Anything else?" the PIE Guy asked yet again.

"I don't know," Clare hissed, starting to sound irritated. "Help me here. I'm running out of ideas."

"How often do you take inventory?" the PIE Guy asked. "How often do you sit down and plan out what you need to do? It can be quite cathartic to put pen to paper or build a spreadsheet that can remove unwelcome surprises, such as a shortage of chocolate chips."

"I suppose that would be useful," Clare responded. "But as you can see, I don't have time to make notes on what is already in my head. Plus, my method usually works well."

"But let's pretend you do have the time," the PIE Guy said. "Let's pretend it's a rainy day and you have very few customers. You're looking for something to do, so you start to write things down that you want to achieve. What benefits would you gain from that? Would you find yourself less stressed in the morning? Would you be better able to manage your staff?"

"I see where you're going with this," Clare replied. "If I wrote things down, I would have a process that would require less time so I could spend more time on the important issues. And I'd also be able to teach my staff to help me instead of doing it all myself, or expecting them to magically know what I need them to do."

"Right you are, Clare!" the PIE Guy exclaimed, clapping her on the back. "This process of writing your ideas down would help you both

mentally and physically to prepare for success. Mentally, because you are now able to free up the capacity and processing power of your brain, and physically, because the stress you experience every morning isn't good for you. Of course knowing this is one thing... you also have to be willing to change."

The PIE Guy looked around at all the members of the group. "We are all resistant to change. It's natural to be resistant to change," he continued. "For example, if you put goldfish in a tank and then put a glass slider down the middle of the tank, the fish will swim in the area you've allotted them. Remove the slider after two days, and the same goldfish will continue swimming in only half the tank.

"We get conditioned by our environment. We accept its boundary conditions and—even in the face of change—we have a natural tendency to continue doing the same things as before. This doesn't mean we're immune to change, but it means we require encouragement to change. Often that encouragement comes in the form of irritants, things that cause us pain in our day or that we're consistently told we need to improve upon. In your case, Clare, the 'pain' may be the need to train others for greater success by articulating what needs to be done, and the first step may be to write things down."

Now turning to Mathew, the PIE Guy asked, "How about you, Mathew? Are you beginning to see an underlying message of PIE? We need to have a mindset that allows the possibility that there is room for personal development. Have you been able to think about what you can do slightly differently now to get a better result in the future?"

"I always achieve my target—that's not the problem. I just never seem to get the promotions when they come up," Mathew responded. "Anyway, like I said yesterday, I think I could turn to my role profile and the feedback I've received from my manager. If I compare what I actually do with what those sources say I should be doing, it might help me identify the things I need to change in order to finally get what I want."

The PIE Guy nodded in agreement. "That's a big part of becoming Prepared. We need to prepare ourselves for greater success. There are so many ways to begin this process, such as looking a level or two above your level in the organization and understanding what is required. This is important if you are looking for a career path. Comparing skills required at the next level with where you are and the skills you have, helps to identify gaps you'll need to overcome. In fact, take a look at the next page on my flipchart," he said, opening it and displaying the page to the group.

"As you prepare to make changes that will help you get to the next step in your career path, these are the key questions you must consider," he said. "Look at where you were ten years ago compared to today. Change happens naturally. We know more today than we did ten years ago. We use this knowledge to our advantage.

"We have a natural force within us that seeks to improve and change, but it takes time and has its own pace. That doesn't mean we can't influence it. We need a mindset for change–we need to ask ourselves questions about it. What do I do well? What do I enjoy doing? What do I constantly avoid doing? What do I not enjoy doing? What causes me the most pain in my day?

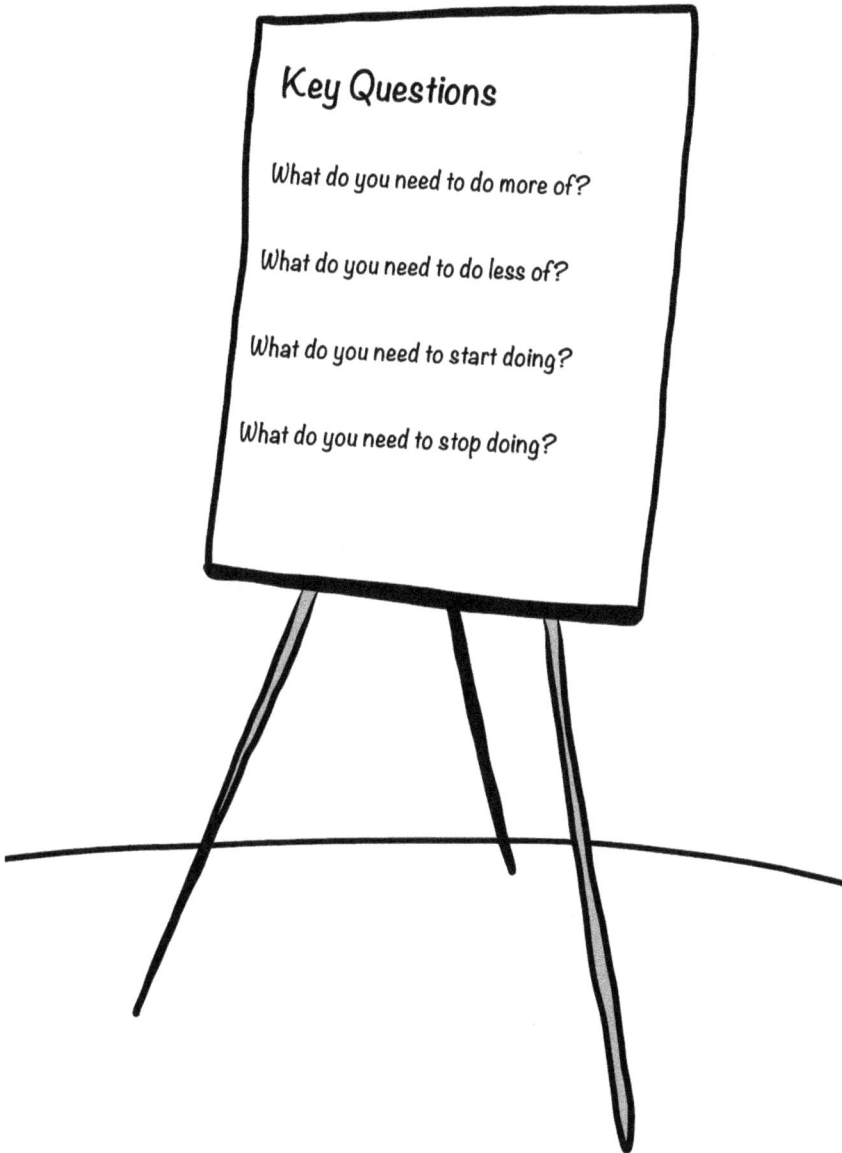

"What do you have to say about that, Toni?" the PIE Guy finished.

"This is easy," she said. "There are things I know I don't do particularly well, so I farm those tasks out for others to do."

"But what happens if there aren't any takers?" the PIE Guy inquired.

"Then I have to find a way to do them myself," Toni responded. "That actually happened recently when we decided we should start marketing our newest technology product through social media. We've mostly relied on word of mouth for growth up until now, and it's served us well. I can write, but I tend to be wordy, and that's not a style that is suited to Twitter or Facebook. So I asked a couple of our younger staff members if they'd like to take it on. They politely declined saying they were already too busy."

"So what did you do?" the PIE Guy asked.

"I went to a social media marketing conference," Toni replied. "In two days I was able to attend several seminars on writing for social media and best practices in social media marketing. Then I went back to the office and drafted our first campaign."

"Nice that you took the initiative, but it doesn't sound very sustainable. You are definitely someone who doesn't like to wait for things to happen. Am I right, Toni?" said the PIE Guy with a smile. "So is there anything that causes you pain in your day or that you've consistently heard you need to improve upon?"

"I think I have the right people, but how I engage them may not be working. Some of my senior leadership team told me I need to slow down and listen to people," Toni replied. "My brain processes things pretty quickly and I usually take the same approach as with social media. I do whatever I need to do to ensure the job gets done, but that's one of the reasons I'm here. I know what I do at times isn't sustainable, especially as the lead on this expansion project into the American market."

The PIE Guy quickly agreed. "Yes, focusing on improving your leadership effectiveness sounds like a better workable plan than increasing your level of individual contribution. Getting your leadership right means having less resistance from your team. Increased employee engagement soon follows. So by asking for feedback from your team and reviewing what is expected of your role, you may be able to focus on what really matters and identify gaps you need to address. This allows you to explore Preparedness through a number of alternate possibilities and ideas."

Turning to Charles, the PIE Guy asked, "What are your thoughts about Preparedness, Charles?"

"We actually learned to prepare in business school," Charles said. "I feel like I had analysis drilled into my head. Basically, we looked at any type of risk or opportunity: market conditions, suppliers, personnel, technology, manufacturing materials and techniques, competition, etc.

"This meant we continued to create a better product or reduce costs in certain areas, which in turn made the company more profitable, or built a better image because of more robust components or a lighter overall product. The list of benefits from the analysis is long, and we have departments and teams of people looking at this stuff," he finished.

"I'm thrilled you mentioned analysis on a company level," said the PIE Guy. "I often suggest to the professionals I work with that this type of business analysis is very similar to the analysis we need to do on ourselves. We need to surround ourselves with people that see us as a 'high-quality racing mountain bike' and help us to understand how we can improve ourselves.

"Back to my main point about analyzing our performance and how we achieve what we achieve. We use new knowledge, acquired from many resources, to make ourselves more robust. This new knowledge, combined with job descriptions, role profiles, and feedback from our line managers, forms a personal analysis that can help us make the most of our talents and opportunities. Just think about it: You are most likely to succeed in life if you use your talents to their fullest extent. Similarly, you'll suffer fewer problems if you understand your weaknesses and manage them so they don't affect the work you do.

"What makes this personal analysis especially powerful is that, with a little thought, it can help you uncover opportunities that you would not otherwise have spotted. And by understanding your weaknesses, you can manage and eliminate threats that might otherwise hurt your ability to move forward. If you look at yourself using this framework, you can start to separate yourself from your peers and further develop the specialized talents and abilities you need to advance your career.

"Let's look at a few questions you can each ask yourself when performing a personal analysis." The PIE Guy walked over to his flipchart and began writing quickly.

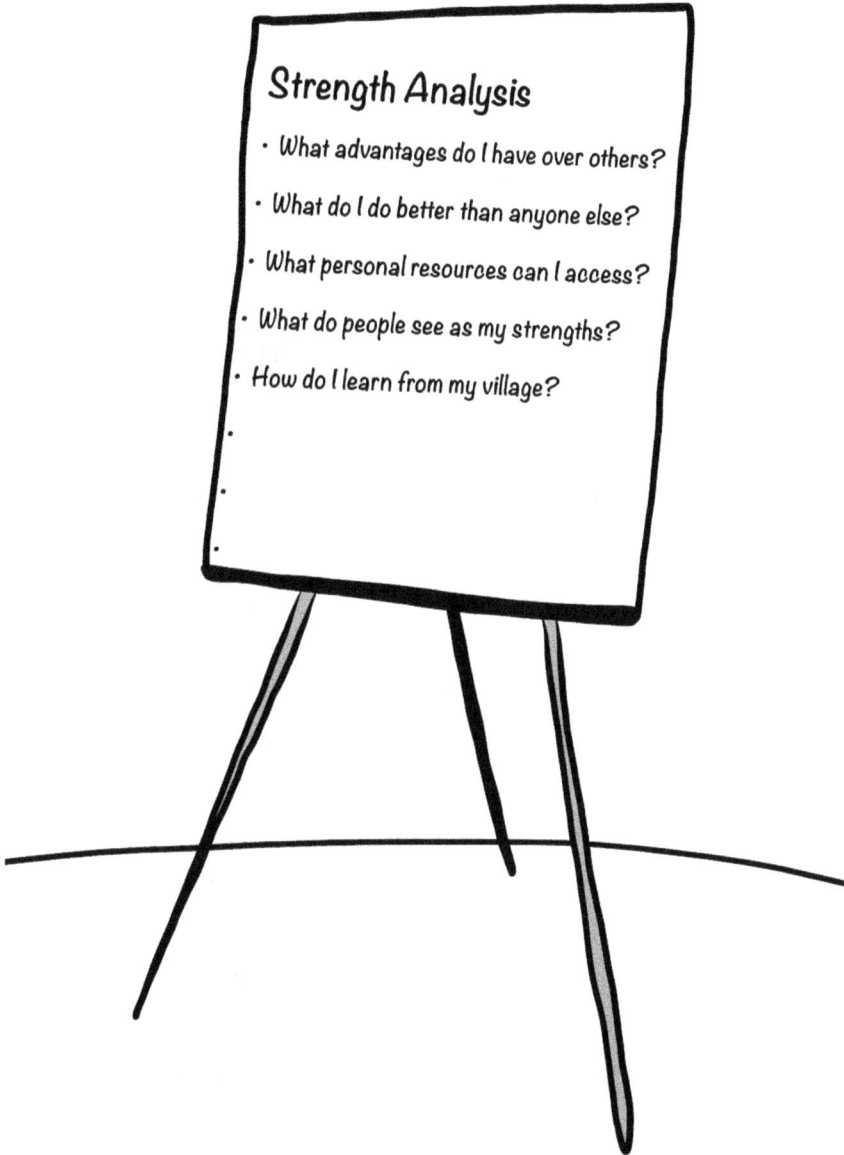

Strength Analysis

- What advantages do I have over others?
- What do I do better than anyone else?
- What personal resources can I access?
- What do people see as my strengths?
- How do I learn from my village?
-
-
-

"Advantages also include skills, certifications, and education," the PIE Guy continued. "You should consider the answers to these questions about strength from your own perspective as well as from the point of view of people around you. Don't be modest or shy. Be as objective as you can. If you identify strengths that are common within your position, for example, a baker who is great at baking, then these characteristics are not considered strengths in your current role—they are actually necessities."

The PIE Guy turned back to Charles to ask him another question. "Charles, can you use the same methods of analysis you perform on your racing bikes to analyze your personal situation?"

"I'll have to think about it," said Charles. "As far as my advantages go, I had a decade of experience as a professional racing mountain biker before getting involved in this company—that's definitely something most other people don't have. I suppose I'm really good at seeing where the company needs to go. I'm better at that than anyone else. And I'm pretty tireless when I'm working. I can go without sleep whenever necessary. Some people consider that one of my strengths."

The PIE Guy replied, "When you spend some time on it, I'm sure you'll come up with even more. It's really important to understand your positive traits. Of course, we also need to look at those that are less desirable and consider how they may be impacting our path to greater success."

Turning to the next page on his flipchart, he continued to write.

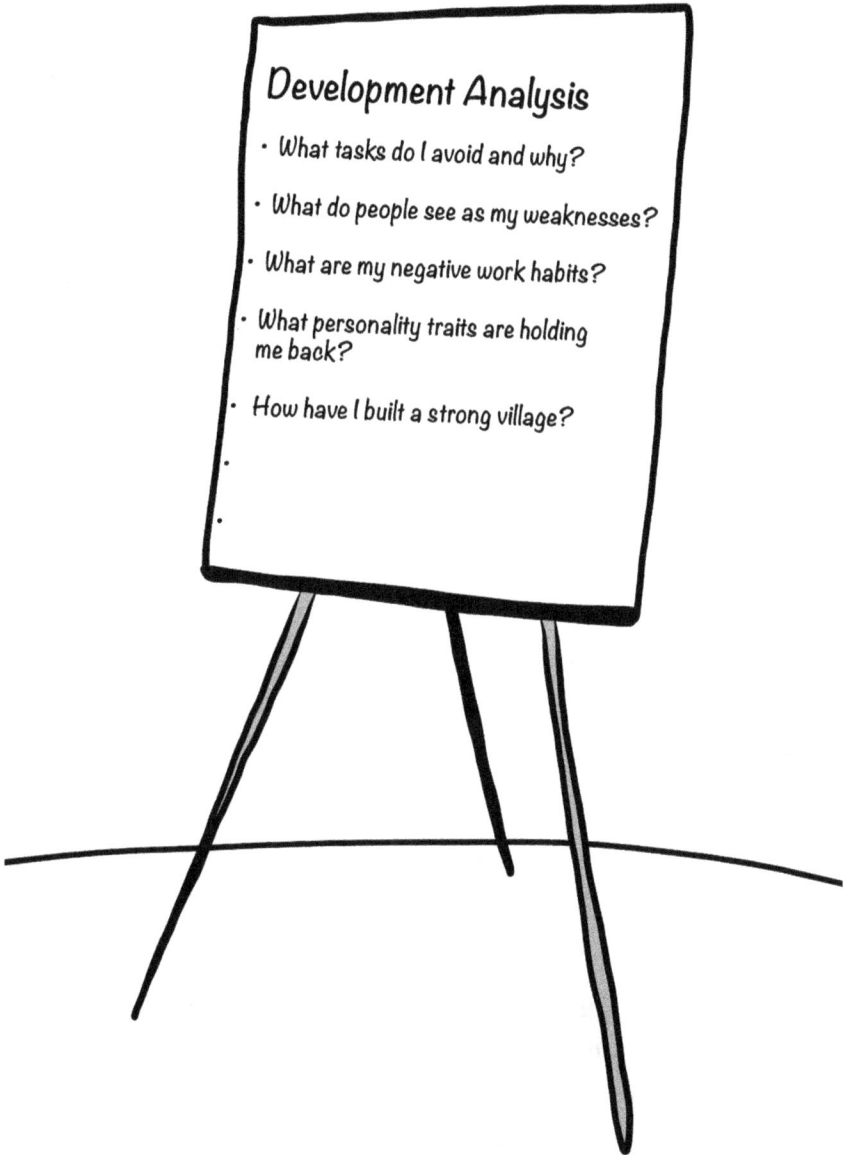

Development Analysis

- What tasks do I avoid and why?
- What do people see as my weaknesses?
- What are my negative work habits?
- What personality traits are holding me back?
- How have I built a strong village?
-
-

"Again, consider these questions from an internal perspective and from an external perspective. Do other people see weaknesses that you don't see? Do coworkers consistently outperform you in key areas? Be realistic—it's best to face any unpleasant truths as soon as possible," the PIE Guy finished, turning to Mathew. "You've been quiet for a while. What are your thoughts?"

"You've mentioned external and internal perspective," Mathew replied. "That isn't something I've considered before. I usually just put my head down and crank out the work I've been asked to do."

"And doing so has helped you rise to the level you've achieved, right?" asked the PIE Guy.

"Well, yes. I've worked quite hard to get to where I am," said Mathew.

"I'm sure you have," said the PIE Guy. "Have you been given the opportunity to lead projects or people?"

"Actually, I prefer to work alone," Mathew said. "It's the only way I can control the results. In the past, when my boss has asked a group of us to collaborate, it has never gone that well for me. My suggestions were usually ignored in favor of what the others suggested."

"Hmmm," the PIE Guy replied. "Collaboration and teamwork can be a big change if you are used to being an individual contributor. Perhaps thinking through the collaborative situations you've been included in could give you ideas on what you could do differently to get better results. Matching the promotion you are looking for with the skills and capabilities required might also help you identify things you can do differently. Does that help, Mathew?"

"I think you are right," said Mathew. "I've been cynical because I've seen so many people get promoted. I've focused on complaining instead of looking at what I am in control of, and making a change if that's what was necessary. I'm starting to see that you and the human resource business partner are only trying to open my eyes to what needs to be done. It's *my* opportunity for growth."

"Welcome aboard!" beamed the PIE Guy. "Here's something else to consider while you're thinking about this: It may help to take a look at the bigger picture—outside your team, department, or company," said the PIE Guy, brandishing a new sketchbook page.

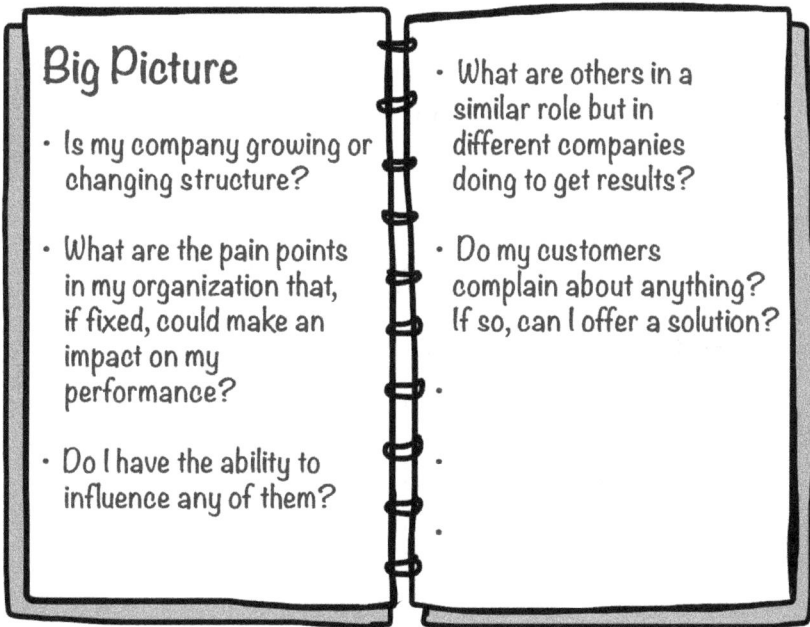

Big Picture

- Is my company growing or changing structure?

- What are the pain points in my organization that, if fixed, could make an impact on my performance?

- Do I have the ability to influence any of them?

- What are others in a similar role but in different companies doing to get results?

- Do my customers complain about anything? If so, can I offer a solution?

-
-
-

"When thinking about opportunities to explore and prepare for your continued success, it helps to make a list of the many possibilities you discover," the PIE Guy said. "Keep performance, process, and people in mind. Networking events, educational classes, conferences, new roles, new projects, new bosses, and company expansions and acquisitions are all opportunities to explore.

"There are so many questions that we can start with to probe and explore what we can change to get better results. Here are a few more for consideration:

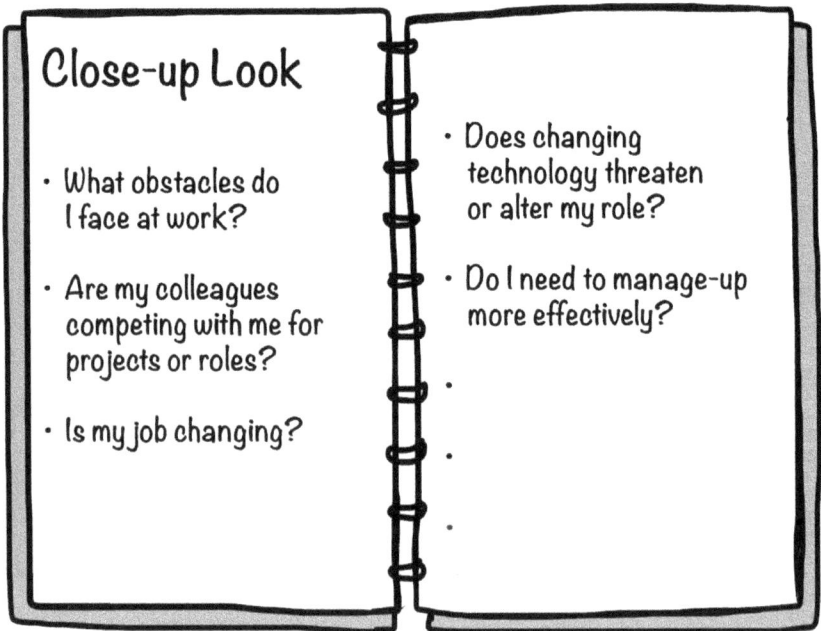

Close-up Look

- What obstacles do I face at work?

- Are my colleagues competing with me for projects or roles?

- Is my job changing?

- Does changing technology threaten or alter my role?

- Do I need to manage-up more effectively?

-

-

-

"Performing this type of analysis will always provide key information. It can point out what you need to do to prepare for success and put any difficulties you're having into perspective," the PIE Guy concluded.

"I must say," Charles chimed in, "the gears in my mind are grinding away faster than before. You mentioned pain points, and those are things I'm used to thinking about in relation to my organization. Pain points are driving our investigation into possible manufacturing expansion to other markets. But I'm realizing I have my own pain points as well, and that is something I don't think I've ever considered before. One of them is how I lead. I have very strong opinions and want to ensure that this company I've invested in survives. As a result, I drive my ideas through my team, rarely soliciting their advice. Perhaps that is something I can work on to get better results."

Toni interjected, "The more I think about it, I believe leadership is my pain point as well. When I worked as an individual contributor, like Mathew, I got amazing results. Then I started managing teams and needed to get results through them. I've done so, but not with the best reviews of my leadership capabilities. Perhaps there is something else here that I need to prepare for as I think about building a senior leadership team in my part of the organization."

"Excellent reflections, Charles and Toni," said the PIE Guy. "Does anyone else have anything to add?"

"I see where you are going with this," Clare said. "And preparedness, as you call it, could help me a bit. But I was thinking you were going to radically change me. After all, it's not that often that people drop into my café from a helicopter!"

"Ha! You are right there!" the PIE Guy enthusiastically agreed. "Perhaps many people don't enter meetings in that way. But there are so many reasons to be in a helicopter. For one, the views are amazing and I could see traffic starting to build on the highways already. I guess it's a bit like what we have been talking about. Sometimes we need to be able to see the big picture to identify trends, and then examine some details to find things we need to change. It's important to get a different view or perspective on things in order to see the opportunities for improvement.

"Oh, and I'll let you in on one secret, Clare. I don't change people—I can't. People have a tendency to change once they are exposed to the concepts we're talking about, but that change comes down to the individual's ability and willingness to improve. The impact I have on your change is similar to that of an executive coach asking questions and helping to carve out your individual development pathway. Whether you decide to take the pathway and continue your personal development to achieve greater success is really up to you."

> **Don't expect others to change you. Empower yourself and decide when change is needed.**

The PIE Guy turned to address the whole group. "Today has been a challenging day filled with questions and conversation. Who can summarize today's learning?"

Clare spoke first, saying, "Preparing ourselves for greater success or living through change requires a fair bit of self-analysis and asking lots of questions. These questions lead to a discovery of where we think we are, where we are, and where we need to be."

"Succinctly put, Clare," stated the PIE Guy. "Does anyone have anything else to add?"

Charles added, "Building on what Clare said, I'd like to add that what we are talking about appears similar to the FEMA example we talked about earlier. Like FEMA, we need to learn the process of building our first Success PIE, and then we should be able to replicate it time and time again, like FEMA would replicate its process in the different scenarios it comes across."

"Right you are, Charles," said the PIE Guy. "Once you have been through the three lessons of Preparedness, Image, and Effort, and once you understand the foundations of building greater success, you'll have the critical components and should be able to replicate improvements time and time again. Why don't we meet here again tomorrow? I'll reach out to Stuart to see if things are okay and give him an update on our discussion," he concluded. "It's kind of funny, but the best conversations tend to take place at cafés!"

CHAPTER 3

I = IMAGE

A rock pile ceases to be a rock pile the moment a person contemplates it, bearing within the image of a cathedral.

Antoine de Saint-Exupery

Keep Your PIE Fresh

"We're not open yet!" Clare called out, turning toward the front of the café the following morning. Most of the group had arrived a few minutes before and were reviewing their notes from the previous day's session.

"It's just me," said Stuart, as he walked in through the door. "Sorry I missed yesterday and am late today. I was on a conference call with my managers about upcoming projects and had too many extra calls. I was tied up telling people what they needed to be doing. The PIE Guy called, but I couldn't take his call so he emailed me with a recap of yesterday's conversation around Preparedness. Thanks, PIE Guy."

The PIE Guy had a quick conversation with Stuart around Preparedness while the rest of the group watched Clare pull freshly baked muffins out of the oven. A delicious fragrance filled the air, and more than one stomach began growling. Unfortunately, Clare did not appear happy with her handiwork.

"Oh no, some of my muffins didn't turn out," she said with a sigh.

"What appears to be the problem with them?" the PIE Guy asked, leaning over the counter to get a better look.

"They just don't look right," Clare responded.

The PIE Guy picked one up, took a bite, and said with a smile, "What does it matter? They still smell and taste great!"

"I'm glad you think so," said Clare, "but how these muffins look actually matters to my customers. They've come to expect muffins with a golden brown exterior and just the right amount of chocolate chips on the surface. Some of these muffins are way too dark, and even though they taste exactly the same, my customers will think they are an inferior product."

"That sounds a lot like the topic for today's conversation," said the PIE Guy, finishing his muffin. "As professionals, our image is part of who we are and how we sell what we sell, whether it's an idea, a collaborative effort, or a change we'd like to make to a process.

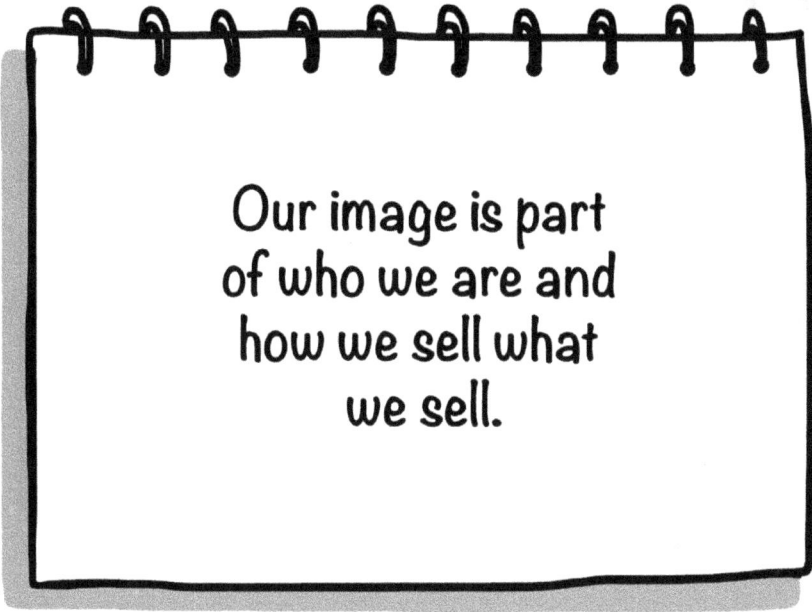

> ## Our image is part of who we are and how we sell what we sell.

"We can define *image* as 'your personal brand.' But unlike your muffins, Clare, image runs deeper than what we see. In the case of the muffins, image would be more like what we see, smell, *and* taste. It's the way people understand who you are, and it's based on the alignment of your attitudes, behaviors, and communication skills to something greater, whether that's your boss, your department/company, your values, or your beliefs. Your image sends powerful but silent messages about you to everyone you encounter or interact with—both at work and outside the office. These messages link directly to your continued success and are something we will talk about later on.

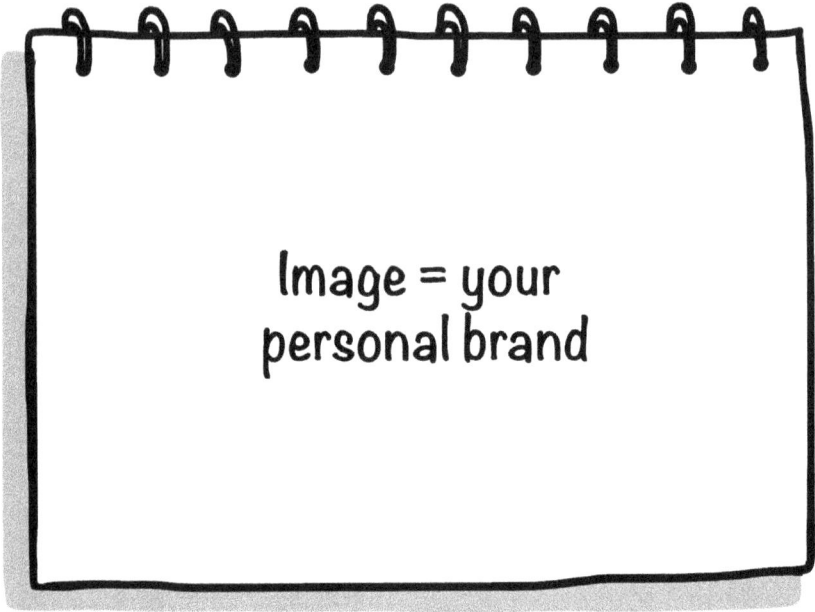

Image = your personal brand

"We can basically divide image into two parts: How you perceive yourself and how others perceive you. These parts need to be in alignment. If you were to write down the top five things that represent you as an individual, and then ask a close colleague or friend to write down the top five things they believe represent you, similarities would indicate alignment. Lack of similarities would mean you have some work to do in the area of image."

Stuart chimed in. "I experienced something similar to this the other day when I was having my monthly one-on-one with my boss," he said. "My success so far has been based on me being a people person, building quick relationships with customers, having a great reputation with my customers, and having a good sales record to add to the mix. However, my boss told me that my recent 360 feedback from my direct reports came back with areas where I need to improve. I was a little confused. I thought I had a good relationship with my teams across the region."

The PIE Guy said, "It's good that your company invests in its leaders through 360 feedback. Not many companies are forward thinking enough to develop their people in this way. It may be helpful to think about this feedback as a type of support that is helping you achieve more success in your role. As you move through different roles in a company, there will be new aspects of the role that you need to learn or a specific skill you need to hone. Just because your feedback offered insight to potential improvement doesn't mean you are doing poorly. It means someone cares about your development enough to give feedback that can help you get to the next level. Were you responsible for people management in your last role?" the PIE Guy queried.

"I had a small local team that were easy to manage. They just wanted to come to work and do their job. There wasn't much more to managing them. We got good results, so that's why I was promoted," said Stuart. "Now I have a regional team with more people. They are geographically spread out and my team has their own teams. My career has taken a big leap forward!"

The PIE Guy was impressed. "Sounds like an exciting career move. There are some things to think about as you read through your 360. Think through the relationships that you had with your previous team and your regional team," said the PIE Guy. "While reading the 360, think about your old team and ask yourself: How well did I know my old team? How did I get to know them? How did we get those results? Was it replicable or lucky?"

Stuart seemed deep in thought. "Hmm, you posed some thought-provoking questions. My old team and I were close, we had a lot of laughs and we got great results. I worked hard developing the

relationships, but that last question you asked has me thinking—was I lucky or good? Isn't that what you were talking about when we first met? I'll need to think it through," said Stuart thoughtfully.

Mathew said, "Now you've got *me* thinking, Stuart. Being lucky or good? Replicating results…and all this talk about what constitutes the best muffin." Mathew chuckled and then said, "All I've ever really had to think about is coming to work well dressed—I just did what came naturally to me."

Image runs deeper than our appearance.

"There may be a few things to think about, Mathew, and physical appearance is only part of the equation," said the PIE Guy. "Like the conversation about muffins, Clare said it's not just the golden brown color, but also the smell, texture, and amount of goodies inside. The physical appearance is important, but so are the intangibles and other aspects of what represents a good muffin. If you're dressing up every day and hitting your financial targets but still not winning that promotion you've been after, it may be worth thinking through the ABCs of image: Appearance, Behavior, and Communication. You also need to think about the perception others have of you. Are you perceived as an individual contributor instead of a leader? Does this limit your advancement?"

Mathew thought for a moment. "Perhaps that's why others have been promoted and I continue to be an individual contributor. I don't feel like a member of a team. I get great results and I have a manager, but it feels like I'm an individual contributor instead of a team member. I suppose you're right," said Mathew. "I've not looked at my career in this way. I think after giving presentations, I get more compliments on whatever tie I'm wearing that day rather than on the content of the presentation I gave. So what else can I do differently to increase my chances for this promotion?" he asked earnestly.

"Perhaps if I ask a few questions, you could think through your situation at work and discover where/what you could do differently to achieve greater results," the PIE Guy responded. "When you are interacting with others at a meeting, networking, or attending a work event, how mindful are you of their experience of the interaction? Are they experiencing what you want them to experience? Do they see you as a collaborator and a person that wants to become a leader?

"In each of your interactions, your peers are creating the image they hold of you. However, *you* are influencing their creation of that image, and those who know how to manage that process will earn the respect of their peers and supervisors.

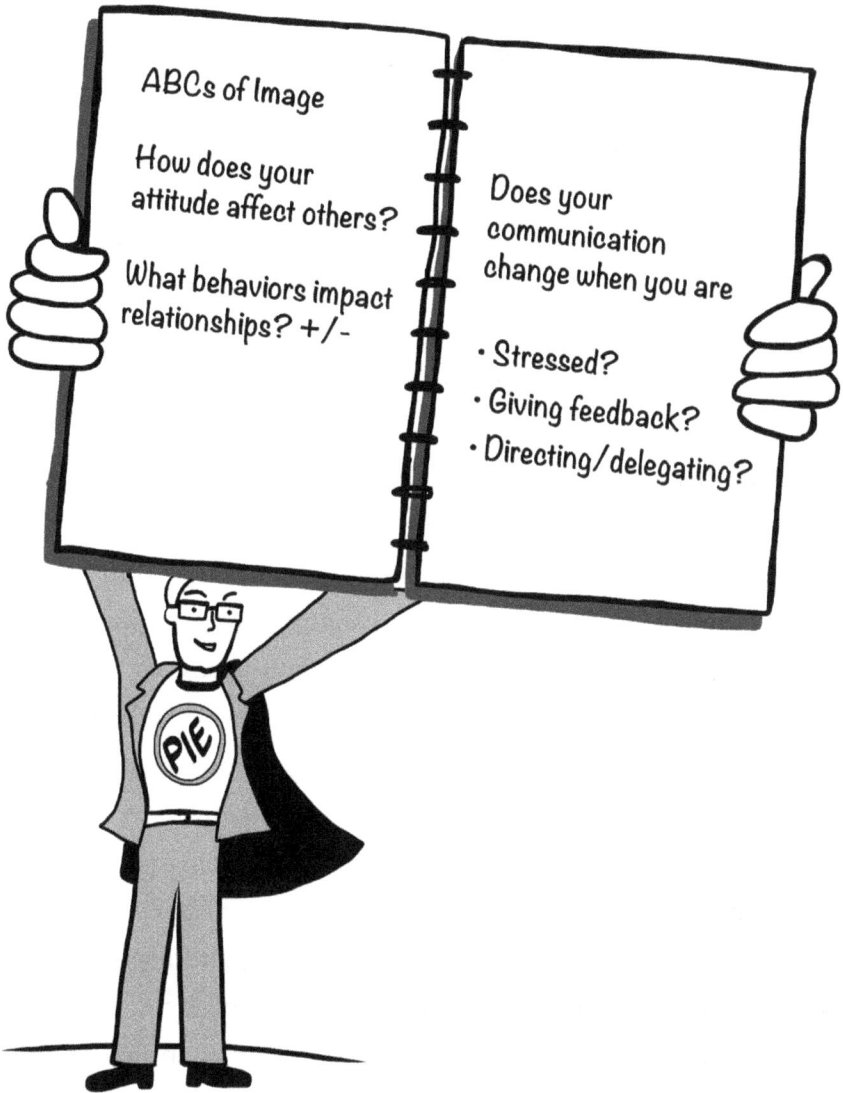

"At first, image building may be a challenge. However, when you start to see yourself living through the 'lens of others,' your perspective will change, and you will become more mindful about how you approach building the image you desire," the PIE Guy concluded.

"Wearing the right clothes hasn't delivered the real result I've been hoping for," said Mathew. "Maybe I need to pretend to be a bit more interested in meetings. You know, act like I'm engrossed in what other people are saying."

"Don't confuse building your image with acting, pretending, or a temporary fix," the PIE Guy said. "Your image should be who you naturally are and want to be so that you can perform at your optimal level. If your boss or colleagues don't understand what image you are trying to create, you need to work harder at creating the image you want them to have of you." Turning to Toni, he asked about her experience with image as an executive.

"I deal with many different people every day," Toni replied, "and I suppose I need to cultivate a slightly different image with each group. For example, when I deal with investors, I have to appear confident when I'm speaking about finance. When I work with our IT department, I have to use my 'geek speak' and interact on their level. When I'm around the rest of my employees, I need to be approachable, but inspiring so I can motivate them to do their best work. And when I'm with potential clients, I need to communicate in terms they can understand while displaying an image that says 'we're the right company for your needs.' It's pretty complicated, and I'm learning based on what we are discussing in this group. I know it's an important part of leadership as well."

"It does sound as though you understand your various stakeholders," the PIE Guy agreed. "What do you think these people are thinking about your leadership when you're working with them? Do you think the image you are trying to create differs in any way from the image they have of you?"

"I'm sure it does," said Toni. "I know for a fact that because I'm so driven, some people have a negative opinion of me. While I see myself as an enthusiastic dreamer who has worked hard to get things done in order to make the world a better place, there are some employees who think I'm selfish, self-important, obsessed, unrealistic, demanding, and focused on winning at all costs."

"That's a lot of feedback to process. How does it make you feel to have such diverse opinions about your image?" the PIE Guy questioned.

"It could be painful if I let it be," Toni replied. "I guess the positive thing is that the feedback has resulted in my attendance here today. I need to ensure that the right people see who I really am. My team is probably the area where my image is not what I would like it to be. We get results, but the results are largely driven by me pushing."

"Their perception is also their reality," said the PIE Guy. "No matter what image you hold of yourself, those with whom you work and interact create their image of you as a leader, employee, colleague, supervisor, spouse, parent, or friend. Socrates once wrote, 'Know thyself.' However, while knowing oneself is important, your ability to understand how others perceive you is an even more powerful tool to help you build greater success."

Toni agreed. "Leadership image is very critical to the success of my business. It's an area I need to explore further."

Image is built one interaction at a time.

The PIE Guy continued on this train of thought. "Interaction is largely the basis of perception. This means you're building your image day by day, one interaction at a time," said the PIE Guy. "You must be constantly aware of how others perceive their interactions with you so you can adapt and adjust as needed. You must 'walk the walk' and not just 'talk the talk.'

"How does image play into your professional situation, Charles?" the PIE Guy asked.

"We use image in our marketing all the time," Charles replied. "Our racing mountain bikes are expensive, but they're also the lightest and strongest available. We use that image to sell them to young racers, but it doesn't work as well on other consumers. Right now, we're trying to come up with a campaign to get more families cycling together, so we're working on creating an image that will appeal to family bikers. I'm seeing strong connections between what we do as an organization and what you are asking us to do on a personal level."

"Great," said the PIE Guy. "But what role does image play in who you are and how you work as the chief operating officer?"

"This is an interesting parallel! There are many similarities between how we market our bikes and how I market myself," said Charles.

"Where could you go to find out others' perception of you?" asked the PIE Guy.

"Well, my wife frequently tells me exactly what she thinks I should focus on," Charles said with a laugh. "But not many others feel free to share, maybe because they see me as one of the big bosses. What do you think?"

"I agree. The higher you go in an organization, the more you'll find yourself surrounded by people reluctant to offer honest feedback," said the PIE Guy. "How could you create an environment that will enable you to receive more balanced feedback?"

"One of my colleagues used a facilitator," said Charles. "She had a person from outside the company collect 360 feedback from her senior team. It worked out well because the facilitator created a safe and confidential environment that allowed my colleague's staff to speak freely about her, especially knowing that what they said would help her become more successful as a CPO, sorry, chief procurement officer."

"Yes, there are always ways to elicit honest feedback," said the PIE Guy. "Sometimes we just need to be creative in how we go about it. How about the rest of you? Who could you approach to learn more about your image?"

"I think I'm going to talk to a few of my colleagues," replied Stuart. "I need to understand if my behaviors or ways that I speak have a negative impact on them. For example, I try to keep things casual—it's kind of the Aussie way. I speak pretty informally to my team and peers, but we don't really joke around like my old team."

"And you suspect this is affecting your image?" the PIE Guy asked.

"The more I think about it now, I'm sure it is," Stuart said. "I knew my old team very well. We knew what each other was thinking before it came out of someone's mouth. We had a laugh as well. I don't know my new team all that well, even though we've been working together for some time now. I don't even know if some have families! This is something I'm going to need to change."

Toni interjected, "Sometimes I hear people murmur or grumble when I leave a meeting, but that doesn't really tell me much. I think I need to talk to the people I know I can trust to tell me the truth, because they want to help me succeed."

"I'm thinking I need to get 360 degree feedback," agreed Mathew. "I'm going to talk to HR and see if they can help. In the past, I've only paid attention to the positive feedback I've received from my line manager. However, now I'm seeing the need to consider the full spectrum of feedback. Maybe, just maybe, I could find some room for improvement," said Mathew with a little smirk.

"I'm glad to hear that, Mathew," said the PIE Guy. "Taking feedback about one's attitudes, behaviors, and communication is rarely easy. People with a false perception of how others see them often rationalize their thinking and defend their ways, saying, 'I'm not really that way. They just don't know who I am.' These people can become defensive and angry, and blame others for their lack of success. It sounds like you're well on your way to avoiding such a situation.

"As we progress in our careers, our image—and others' expectations of us—is likely to change. For example, if you're an individual contributor and you want to be seen as a team player, perhaps you could shift your image to be more collaborative. If you desire to move from a supervisor to a leader, your image will need to change from being a manager to a leader of people.

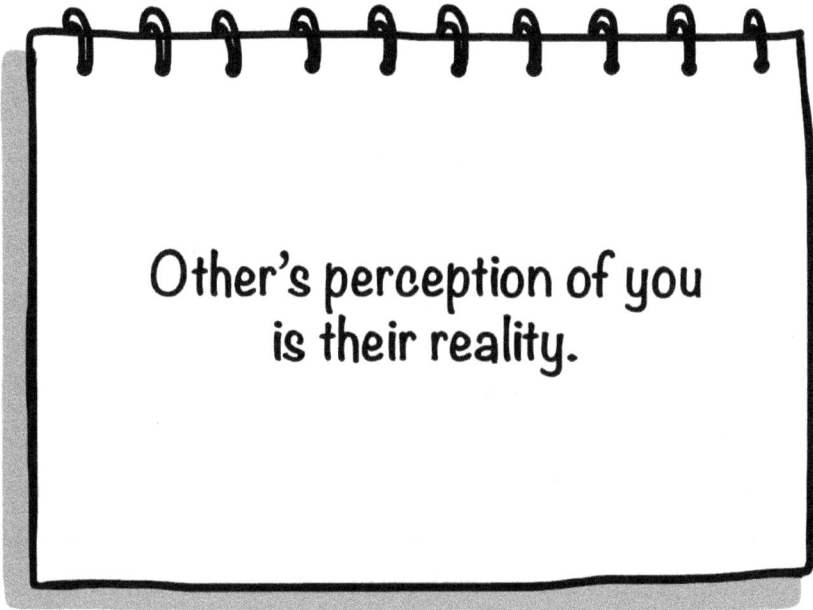

> # Other's perception of you is their reality.

"I've worked with many leaders who confuse getting results with a good image. If their team meets their sales numbers, or wins new clients, or takes things to the next level, they assume everyone sees them positively as a result. But which person would you want to work with: Someone one who has focus, understands the vision, and takes the time to answer your questions, or someone who treats you like a process or a chess piece that needs to be managed?

"In these situations, and all the others like them, it's our image that matters. It's made up of softer skills that form the bedrock of our perception. While technical skills may get your foot in the door, your people skills are what create most of the opportunities in your future. Your work ethic, your attitude, your communication skills, your emotional intelligence, and a whole host of other personal attributes are the soft skills that are crucial for your Success PIE," the PIE Guy concluded.

Charles responded, "I've had to let several people go from my company in the past because they didn't understand this important concept. They thought that as long as they had the technical knowledge and drive to do their job, soft skills didn't matter. But they needed a good grasp on soft skills to excel in their role. Problem solving, delegating, motivating, and team building are essential skills requiring good soft skills. Knowing how to get along with people—and displaying a positive attitude—is always crucial for greater success."

"I agree, Charles," said the PIE Guy. "Unfortunately, many businesses focus on technical skills over soft skills, and there is far less training provided for soft skills as a result. Sometimes there is an assumption that soft skills are universally known or are somehow embedded in our brain. This is not the case, and a lack of soft skills can lead others to form an image of you that doesn't quite match your own perception.

"That's why as a leader, it's important to focus as much on people/soft skills training and development as you do on traditional hard skills. In a few days, as we begin to consider pulling all of this together, you will have the ability to prioritize and decide what to focus on when building your first Success PIE," the PIE Guy concluded.

Wrapping up the day's conversations, the PIE Guy said, "I think it's time to get out of Clare's hair for the day. Who would like to recap what we've covered?"

"I would," said Charles. "To recap, you should now understand the importance of knowing how people perceive you and how that image relates to building success. Others' perception of you is their reality, but it's your responsibility to manage that image.

"How you perceive yourself is important—of course—and it can help give you confidence, but how others perceive you will have a more direct impact on what you can achieve. The gap between what you believe is your image and what others actually experience is an opportunity for improvement. When your perception of your image is out of alignment with how others perceive you, you have the ability to analyze the need to adjust or correct through a series of actions built into your Success PIE," he finished.

"Nicely recapped, Charles," said the PIE Guy. "Let's spend a few minutes capturing what resonated with us today."

"Can I share something with the group first?" Mathew asked.

The PIE Guy nodded.

"When Stuart was talking about how he knew his old team really well and that they laughed quite a lot, I realized I may actually be the opposite. These three-piece suits and my preference for working alone might be adversely impacting my ability to develop collaborative relationships at work. I think I might need to learn to be a bit more relaxed in the office and show I'm willing to get to know my coworkers. I also need to collaborate with them more. The same could help with certain clients—like the younger millennials, who prefer a more informal approach to everything, including their finances."

"Excellent insight, Mathew," said the PIE Guy. "It's good to see the wheels of change grinding away in your mind. I'm looking forward to seeing how this develops tomorrow. Let's meet back here as soon as Clare opens the doors. Then we can take a bite out of our next PIE ingredient."

CHAPTER 4

E = EFFORT

"Opportunity is missed by most people because it is dressed in overalls and looks like work."

Thomas Edison

The PIE Guy arrived at Café Creo Prosperitas shortly after it opened. As he entered the front door, he closed his eyes briefly and inhaled deeply, enjoying the delicious aroma of fresh roasted coffee mingled with the mouth-watering fragrance of Clare's delicious muffins. He walked to the back corner table where the majority of his group was already seated with notebooks, coffee, and—in most cases—muffins in hand.

"Thank you all for making the effort to get here this morning," he said before taking a seat at the table, waving to Clare, who was still behind the counter. "I appreciate the sacrifice of personal time you're making to join me for a discussion of the third key element of every Success PIE. Who remembers what it is?" he asked.

"Effort!" the group announced in unison.

"Right you are!" he exclaimed. "Gold stars all around. Effort is the 'so what am I going to do now?' phase—or the execution phase—of your Success PIE." He paused for a moment and stood to welcome Clare, who was accompanied by a young Indian woman.

"Nimmi! I'm so glad you could join us," he said, drawing her toward the group. "Everybody, this is Nimmi Gupta, one of my international coaching clients. We've been working on her Success PIE together. She's at about the same point in the journey as the rest of you, and the process is really the same, whether you're being coached as a group or individually."

"Thanks for letting me join the group," Nimmi said as she addressed the gathered professionals. "I'm in the country to meet with sponsors of my non-profit organization, and it was the perfect opportunity to meet the PIE Guy in person. I'm looking forward to learning more about PIE along with you for the next several days."

> ## Knowledge is useless unless applied, which takes Effort.

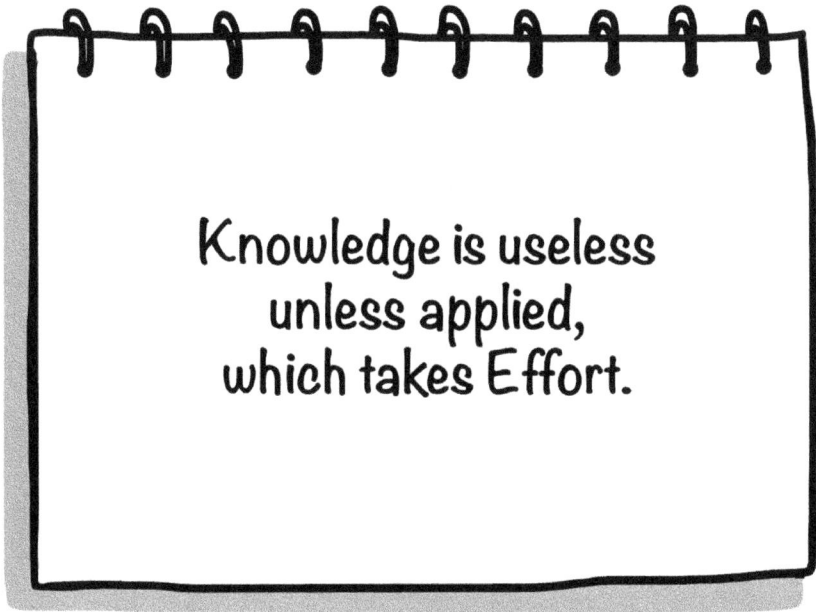

Nimmi and Clare pulled chairs up to the table and sat down as the PIE Guy began. "Getting here this morning took effort. But you all made the effort because you found our development group important enough to do so. When thinking about doing things slightly differently to get a better result, what do you think about when it comes to Effort?" the PIE Guy asked.

"For me, I definitely think about time," said Toni, "and energy, of course. I know it's going to take a fair amount of mental energy to make some of the changes I've been thinking about. I'm not patient, so I know I'll get frustrated along the way."

"Time and energy are always two elements of effort that rise to the top of this discussion," said the PIE Guy. "How about someone else?"

Stuart said, "Scheduling time to get to know my team better is at the top of the list for me."

Effort Takes Many Forms:
- Time Management
- Prioritzation
- Energy
- Honesty
- Strategic / Tactical Thinking
- Learning
-
-
-

Charles chimed in. "I'm thinking more about delegation. I always thought I was delegating, but now I see that I have really been directing, telling people what needs to be done and how to do it. This is important for me…as well as reviewing what I want to do against what I actually do."

"Reviewing our progress is certainly on the list of topics we're going to cover," the PIE Guy agreed. "We will cover this when we talk about the second foundation of PIE. Thanks for thinking ahead, Charles. What does Effort mean for you, Nimmi?"

Nimmi replied, "Again, time and strategic thinking are keys for me. I sometimes get locked into the here and now."

"The 'here and now' can easily occupy a substantial portion of our weeks," said the PIE Guy. "Carving out time for strategic thinking can help maintain a better balance."

"I'm afraid I'm looking at some really big changes," Mathew interjected. "Last night I reflected on a few things I need to do. They're going to require a fundamental shift in how I work."

"Fortunately, you don't have to make huge changes," the PIE Guy reassured. "Personal change really comes in two classifications: first order change or second order change. First order change is what we are talking about with PIE. It's doing things slightly differently to get better results. This is generally achievable alongside your day job.

"Second order change requires a radical rethink about who you are. It often requires you to make vast changes to get on a better path to achieve better results. Mathew, perhaps you could slice your PIE into smaller pieces and prioritize the ones you need to work on first. Sometimes the changes we face are easier to achieve if we break them down into bite-sized pieces.

"This is a great opportunity to have a quick chat about change. There is a natural cycle we all go through when we consider it, and it is quite fascinating. You can compare it to a roller coaster. First we get excited about the prospect of improving. Then we realize that it's going to take work to do so. At that point, our motivation and happiness may decline until we start experimenting with solutions and putting into practice what we know is the right thing to do.

"Eventually, our happiness is greater than it was in the beginning because we understand the process to improvement, and we can initiate a new PIE at will—anytime. Does that help, Mathew?" the PIE Guy asked. "Some changes require vast amounts of effort or energy while other changes require a daily reminder. The important thing to remember is that it is action, not intention, that helps us achieve the results we desire.

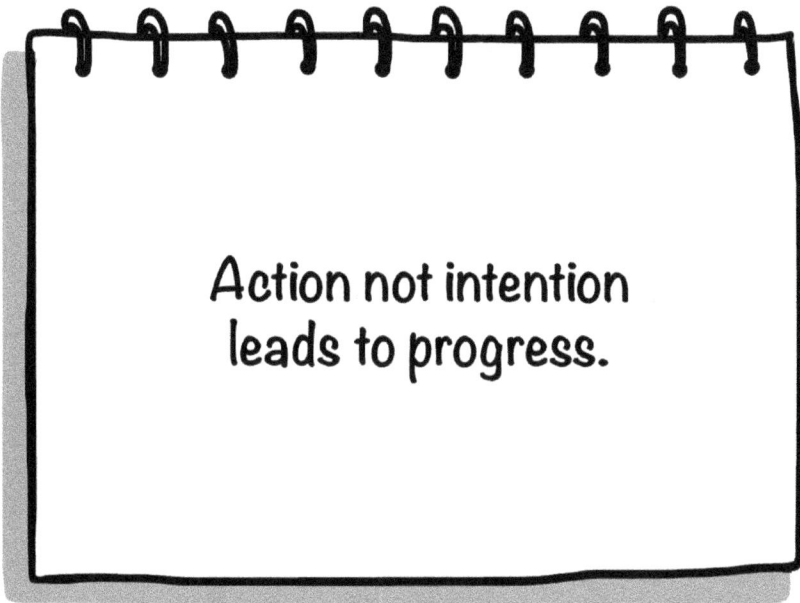

Action not intention leads to progress.

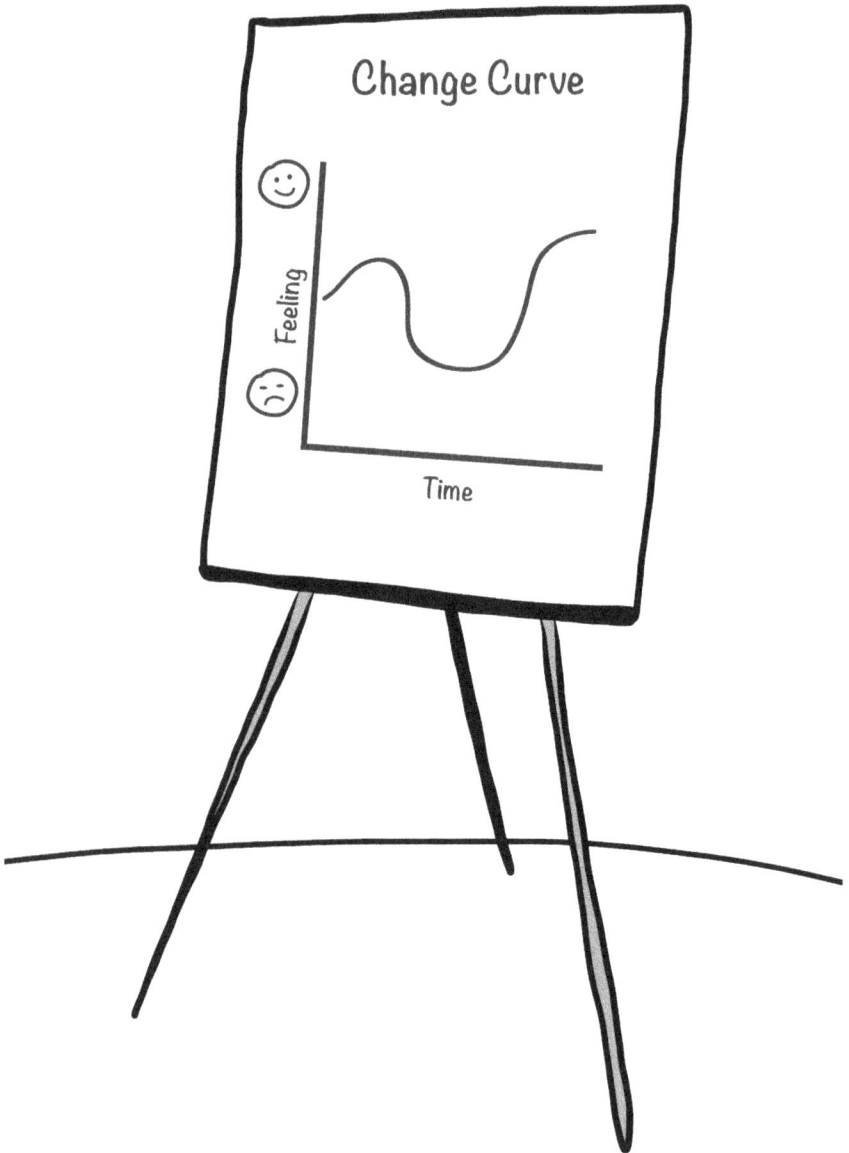

"Remember when we talked about why you do what you do? This question is also critical when thinking about effort—the answers are the things that will keep you motivated. Without proper motivation, it's all too easy to get overwhelmed in the process or to let obstacles—big or small—prevent you from accomplishing what needs to be done in order for you to achieve greater success.

"To move forward, we overcome obstacles. Sometimes the effort feels more challenging than the benefit you'll get for overcoming the obstacle. It's important to make your reason for change bigger than the obstacle. Likewise, you may need to make the effort you have to take to get there more manageable.

"Remember what Clare said near the beginning of our time together? 'We must stop making excuses about why we can't make the necessary changes and turn our attention to why we can't afford *not to* make them,'" the PIE Guy concluded, turning to Clare.

> # Don't let your tasks or performance indicators get in the way of developing yourself.

"Remember when we talked about what would happen if you were unable to get to the café early one morning?" the PIE Guy asked.

Clare nodded. "My customers wouldn't have any coffee or muffins and my business would suffer, and consequently it would affect my family's ability to pay our mortgage," she stated. "My effort is around finding time to plan, and better yet, to build my Success PIE, which incorporates writing procedures so I can train my staff to follow them when I'm not around."

"Think about what could happen if you were forced to be out sick for an entire week," the PIE Guy added. "Suddenly, the importance of writing those procedures seems more important than the obstacle of finding time!"

Lessons learned are not always the best timed.

"You're right," Clare said. "I haven't taken a sick day—or a vacation with my family—since opening the café. In fact, I've worked every single day—except Christmas and New Year's, when we're closed—for the last three years. I've worked on my daughters' birthdays. I've worked on my wedding anniversary. I sent my husband and children to Disney World but I couldn't go with them. All because I just didn't make time to prepare someone else to take my place. Sometimes I feel married to my job instead of to my husband.

"When I think about what I've missed because I was so caught up in the moment, it sickens me. I guess I thought the success of the café was all me, not realizing I had created a village around me that could support and help me. All I needed to do was ask, and prepare them for success by creating a few procedure manuals. What I've missed because of my arrogance and lack of trust—it makes me feel ill," she said.

"The lessons we learn are not always best timed!" said the PIE Guy. "You cannot change the past, but you can certainly change the future. I suspect that at the appropriate time you may reprioritize a few things to bring people along on your journey. And before you know it—if you keep making that effort a priority—you'll be taking days off to spend time with your family, your real family, not your business family.

"While the day-to-day tasks of running your café are essential, you cannot let your task list prevent you from making efforts that will eventually enable you to enhance your success," he concluded.

"What I'm learning," Nimmi interjected, "is that we will always have more than one thing we need to do, more than one goal to strive for, more than one demand placed on our time, but by making the effort to sort and prioritize, we can make more impactful progress, and faster."

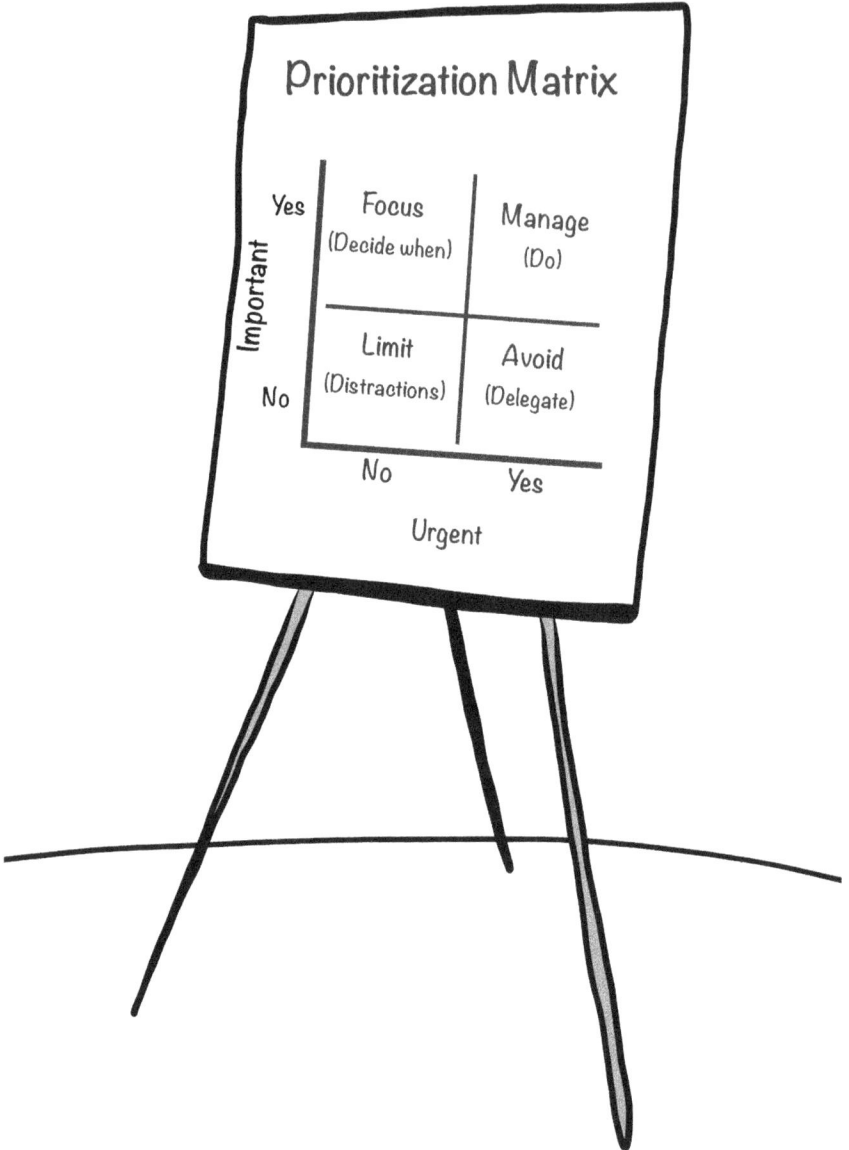

Prioritization Matrix

	No	Yes
Yes (Important)	Focus (Decide when)	Manage (Do)
No	Limit (Distractions)	Avoid (Delegate)

Urgent

"I agree," said Charles. "If something is not that important in the scale of things, put the task low on the priority list. Tasks that align with the larger picture of what we are trying to achieve should take precedence."

"That's spot on, you two," said the PIE Guy. "Next, review your important task items and prioritize them according to their level of importance. How successful are you in dealing with these tasks? If you find actions that are 'stagnating' on your list, consider whether you should re-evaluate their importance or raise their priority level.

"You'll need to review and update your task list periodically. You may want to do so every week. Delete or archive tasks you've completed, add new items, and reprioritize where needed.

"How about you, Stuart?" the PIE Guy continued. "What's the first obstacle you need to tackle? Where do you want to start putting your effort?"

"Well, I mentioned I want to get to know my team better. I'm going to spend time getting to know them on my travels, making sure we spend time talking about business, their development, and life outside work," he reflected. "I'm sure this will help me to build the image I want and create a stronger team that has a bit of a laugh from time to time."

"Yes, where Clare's obstacle can be solved by organizing and prioritizing her efforts, yours appears to be more a matter of scheduling time with your team," the PIE Guy said. "Is there anything else you've seen other leaders do with their teams to create a higher performing team?"

Stuart paused to consider the PIE Guy's question. "Thinking about it now, I see a couple of options. First, I've got a regional conference coming up and I'll use this event as a way to focus on the big three priorities that a previous manager told me about: people, process, and performance. Second, I want to foster a stronger team, so I need to think through some type of rotation or collaboration where my team works more closely together, supporting one another instead of competing. I think there's more I can do in this space, but that seems good for now."

"Excellent!" the PIE Guy exclaimed. "What effort do you need in your situation, Mathew?"

"I've said it before and I'll say it again, I'd like to get another promotion," Mathew said. "But overall, things aren't that bad for me right now. I have time to get my work done. I probably have some spare time to make things easier for my boss, and I still enjoy evenings, weekends, and the occasional vacation with my family."

"Sounds like things are primarily going well for you," said the PIE Guy. "But the desire to be recognized for your hard work is what drove you here. Are you letting go of being recognized with a promotion?"

"Probably not, but I'm starting to get a better idea of what I need to do differently and why I need to do things differently," Mathew replied. "For one thing, I'm always worried that if I don't develop professionally, other people at the company are going to continue to pass me by. And sooner or later, I'm going to become less valuable and less effective in my career."

RISING STAR

SHOOTING STAR

SUPER STAR

"Super Stars are often passed in their career by Rising Stars and Shooting Stars when they allow themselves to stop developing," said the PIE Guy. "It's a good thing that you're already learning what you can do to prevent yourself from being passed."

"As an individual contributor, no one can touch my results," Mathew said proudly. "I am the best the company has at doing what I do. However, I'm only seen as that—an individual contributor.

I've been thinking about the people I've met in this group. It has really opened my eyes. I think that if I want to advance, I need to become more of a team player and share my success with others at the company."

"Collaboration is a core component if you are part of a team," the PIE Guy agreed. "So what are you specifically looking at doing?"

"I think I'll ask my boss if I can set up some internal training sessions to share my techniques," Mathew replied. "I'm also going to change my wardrobe when I'm in the office. While many of my clients expect formality, I think business casual attire will help me better connect with my coworkers."

"It sounds like some great thinking has gone into this," said the PIE Guy. "I especially like how you're incorporating addressing the needs of others—in this case, your boss and colleagues—into how you can advance your own success. Remember in the beginning of the week, I mentioned village as being a foundation of PIE. This is what you are doing, Mathew. Well done. Later in the week we will dive deeper into incorporating others into our success."

"I'd like to hear what you think about my situation," Charles interjected. "It feels pretty complicated, because I have to decide what personal effort to make, but I realize this could have a significant impact on my company as well."

"That does appear to add a level of complexity," agreed the PIE Guy. "Perhaps you could elaborate and share what's on your mind."

"Well, I know I need to make some changes to lead slightly differently to get better results, but we are also trying to decide if we should expand the manufacturing of our bikes to other countries, or if we should remain a UK-only focused company. Will focusing on this personal change alongside the company's change just confuse people?"

The PIE Guy answered, "PIE is an iterative process. Sometimes we identify something that we would like to do differently in one of the areas of PIE, and then we realize that we need to revisit another area to ensure we are successful in making the change. In this instance, it sounds exactly like what you are facing. You know you want to make changes in your perceived Image in how you lead, but you are realizing that you may need to Prepare the path in front of you to help people understand that you are working on becoming a better leader. You don't want your team to be surprised when you try something new during such a critical decision point for the future of the company. Another big benefit to Preparing the path and letting people know you are working on your leadership image is the support and understanding they may offer while you work on becoming a better leader!" the PIE Guy exclaimed. "Visualize engaging your team in the decision-making process and relying on their subject matter expertise. What effect would your leadership mind-set shift have on the rest of your team? How important is it for you to be seen as a good leader as your company continues their next steps in the journey?" he concluded.

"That's a lot to think about, and I'm beginning to see how the leadership style changes I'm considering will have a positive effect on the business decisions we need to make in the near future," said Charles.

"It really comes down to a few simple decisions," the PIE Guy replied matter-of-factly. "Are you going to do something slightly different to get better results or not? Then, are you going to try this on your own or with the support of others? We've touched base on it several times this week and tomorrow we will be diving into this very topic: our village. Our village refers to how those around us can help us to achieve even more than we can on our own. For some of the business and personal decisions you have to make, you can seek the council and support of others during your decision-making process. This could be one of the steps you take to becoming a better leader at work. It wouldn't hurt to start compiling a list of positives you might experience from shifting your leadership style. It could help to overcome the challenges and obstacles you may face as you change your leadership style." Turning to Toni he said, "You're in a similar boat as Charles, as you also have many people depending on you."

"The more we talk about it, the more I think my effort is linked to my image, which is being driven by what I need to do differently as a leader to get better results," Toni said. "I learned a long time ago how to use my type A personality to my advantage. I guess I've been relying on successful techniques of the past to serve me well as I expand this company across international borders. Seems like I can't just keep doing what I've been doing."

"I agree, Toni," said the PIE Guy. "Your rise in the organization will most likely require different skills or at the least skills you need to hone. Switching from an individual contributor or a team member to a leader creates challenges and new requirements. Didn't you say that you had to take a course on social media because your younger staff members were too busy? As a team member or individual contributor, this is an acceptable strategy in adding value. However, I would challenge whether this was an effective use of your time.

As a leader, you can't afford to be an expert at everything. Trusting and relying on your team and providing them with a vision they can align to may be where your time is better placed."

"And I thought I was a quick thinker," chuckled Toni. "I'd really like to keep the staff small while growing the business. I also want to remain the central orchestrator of everything, but I know I'm going to have to add more people to my team. I'm going to need more infrastructure as a result. One place I'll have to put my effort into is in determining how to organize the teams, and place key people in key roles so that they can help me prepare for, and handle, the growth we're going to experience as we expand."

"I think you're on the right track, Toni," said the PIE Guy. "Now, let's hear about Nimmi's experience running a non-profit."

"I've always had a pretty good handle on Preparedness and Image," Nimmi began. "Without having a comprehensive vision of what needs to be accomplished, I wouldn't have been able to accomplish anything—including the great relationships I have with all of the major stakeholder groups inside and outside of my organization, which is a direct link to the image they have of me.

"Prioritizing effort is where I find most of my challenges. I always have about a million things to do, from finding peer companies to gift their time, to make donations, and to fund events, to working on my personal development with the PIE Guy. But I tend to be reluctant to delegate. I try to do everything myself and make everything a priority. As a result, nothing really is a priority," she finished.

"And what is one problem this has caused for you?" the PIE Guy asked.

"One thing?" Nimmi paused a moment to think. "Volunteer turnover is too high. By spreading myself too thin, I've neglected our volunteers," Nimmi replied. "We're a non-profit and I rely on my volunteer army to get things accomplished, and we don't have a lot of money to put toward developing this critical team of volunteers. However, I know I need to find a way to develop them so they feel engaged and valued and want to continue volunteering for the organization. I need to create the dedicated Volunteer Army—that is in my vision for the organization.

"This Volunteer Army is really the key to our work. Without them, we would be nothing. I'd love to find a way to use PIE to help them, but I don't have much time and I have even fewer resources," she concluded.

"So time and resources are your obstacles," said the PIE Guy. "What would you do if you could overcome them?"

"I would have more time if I found someone who could help spearhead the fundraising efforts and build our financial resources," Nimmi replied. "Then I could use the time that was freed to focus on developing my Volunteer Army. You might be surprised, but most of my volunteers don't quit because they lose interest in the cause. They tend to leave because they are tired of the lack of organization and forward planning for the work they are performing.

"If I had more time, I could help build the vision and implement it to help organize our efforts, and celebrate more instead of surviving week by week, wondering if we are going to be able to support the various projects we have on the go," she stated.

"You know what needs to be done, Nimmi, and it's beginning to come together. The next few sessions will definitely help," said the PIE Guy. "We've had some really good conversations about PIE today. Next, we're going to explore how the people around us hold the key to much of the success we experience, and the importance of letting them know about our Success PIE.

"But before we all take off, let's review the main points we've learned about Effort. First, we discussed how you get started. Do you remember what we determined, Clare?" he asked.

"Getting started requires commitment and putting aside the excuses of why you can't make a change, and focusing instead on why you cannot afford *not* to make a change," she replied.

"Excellent. Then we talked about where we should put our efforts," the PIE Guy said. "How do we figure that out, Stuart?"

"We figure out what our obstacles are or what might help accelerate our success," Stuart responded.

"Wonderful. And how do we prioritize the efforts we need to make, Charles?" the PIE Guy asked.

"We start with the ones that are most in alignment with the larger goals we're trying to achieve," Charles stated. "And we look for a few quick wins to keep us motivated."

"Fantastic!" the PIE Guy proclaimed. "Remember, progress is progress, even if it's just small steps. If you can devote one hour a week toward your Success PIE, you'll be well on your way to achieving your goals. Celebrate what you accomplish in that hour and you'll keep the momentum rolling.

> Even small steps
> are progress.

"I look forward to seeing you all here again on Wednesday. Let's meet at noon and chat about our village while we have lunch," he said as he stood and gathered his things. Then, with a quick twirl of his cape, he was gone.

CHAPTER 5

SUCCESS REQUIRES A VILLAGE

No person is an Island, entire of itself;
every person is a piece of the Continent,
a part of the main.

John Donne

Ham and Swiss on rye, curried tofu with vegetables, veggie burger and fries, spinach salad with grilled chicken, a protein shake, and a tuna sandwich—these were just some of the healthy and organic meals provided by Café Creo Prosperitas. The selections were as diverse as the individuals in the PIE Guy's personal development group.

The group members sat at their usual table and chatted amicably as they waited for their coach to arrive. At noon—on the dot—he burst through the café door, resplendent as usual in tweed, colorful spandex, and a swirling cape.

"What a beautiful day!" he called out, almost skipping toward their table, sketchbook in hand. As Stuart pulled out a chair for him, he settled upon it gracefully. "How many people are in your network?" he asked the group. They began doing mental calculations.

"What if I asked how many people are in your village?" the PIE Guy said. "Does anyone know what the difference is between a network and a village?"

"I'll hazard a guess," Charles said. "I'm from a country full of villages, so I imagine networks are big and villages are small."

"Yes," said the PIE Guy. "Back in the day, people used to collect business cards from people they met at various events. This was how they grew their network and demonstrated their value, by the number of business cards they had stashed in their rolodexes. In today's terms, that's like being on LinkedIn and trying to get as many connections as possible.

"While there's nothing wrong with that as a strategy, and it might even work exceptionally well in certain circumstances, a network of acquaintances—or even a virtual network of strangers—is not the same as a village. A village is much more intimate because you know the people in it. You know where they spent their last vacation and you know the names of their spouses and children. You've spent time with them. You want to help them, and they want to help you. And one of the things they'll want to help you with is your PIE.

> # Village members have a vested interest in you and you have a vested interest in them.

"One of the key factors in PIE is working with your village. This group of key people will need to know what you're working on and how you want them to be included in your growth. You can help them grow as well. Unlike a network, in which most people are only thinking about their own benefit, a village is comprised of people who support us and who we support as well.

"How many of you previously believed that the success you had achieved up to this point in your career was purely due to your own motivation, drive, or luck?" the PIE Guy asked.

Several of the group raised their hands.

"If we think about that question and unpack it, we find that our efforts were most likely combined with some other factors that led to our success," he continued. "In the corporate sector, often our line manager gives us an opportunity to do something or to try something new. We apply knowledge and effort to achieve a result, and our line manager then recognizes us for it.

"In a small business or as a sole proprietor, it's not too dissimilar. Instead of a line manager giving us an opportunity, it may be a client that gives us that chance. No one's success is entirely linked exclusively to his or her own abilities. In fact, it's quite often based on opportunities they were given—by someone else—to achieve.

"From teachers and professors in our education system to the employer who takes a chance when hiring us, these opportunities come from many directions. Learning, growing, achieving, and succeeding do not happen in a vacuum, and the quicker we realize that it takes multiple people to help us reach our goals, the quicker we can put this valuable resource to good use," he concluded.

Nimmi chimed in, "I understand. Not only is it valuable to have people in our lives who genuinely care about us and who are there when we need advice, it is also important to have someone to listen to our thoughts, someone to keep us on the right path, someone to help us see a different picture, and someone to encourage us to try again when we've fallen down. It's also important to give these things back as well. The people we successfully do this with constitute our village."

"That's correct," the PIE Guy agreed. "Today we're going to explore the blending of what we've discussed about Preparedness, Image, and

Effort with the needs of these people around us. Where these things meet is a critical part of success. If you have a handle on the first three but neglect the last, you're unlikely to ever achieve your full potential.

> # Investment is a reciprocal relationship when it comes to village members.

"Of course, first you need to figure out exactly who your village members are. Look for people who will give you backing, assistance, advice, information, protection, and even friendship. These individuals will become your support base. As you build strong, professional, personal, and mutually beneficial relationships with them, you will find yourself achieving goals more quickly and smoothly than ever before," the PIE Guy said.

"So we may find village members among our work colleagues, friends, family, and club members," Charles chimed in. "Some are natural choices. They may share a common interest with us, like the colleague who has been around for years and can offer the invaluable voice of experience, or the club member who is always happy to be a sounding board for our ideas."

"Yes," agreed the PIE Guy. "These people naturally become your village members. However, you can find allies in unexpected places, too."

Turning to a new page on his flipchart, he continued. "Mapping your village can be a helpful way to figure out who your villagers are," he stated, showing them the chart he had drawn on a fresh page. It was comprised of a horizontal and vertical axis labeled "Feel About You" and "Vested Interest." There was also a smiley face and a frowny face.

The group members' expressions were quizzical and interested.

"The vertical axis illustrates how people who deal with you on a daily basis feel about you. If they like you, they'll fall into a quadrant with the smiley face on the top. If they are more neutral or don't like you, they'll go in a frowny face quadrant on the bottom. The horizontal axis illustrates whether these people have a low or high vested interest in you. As you think about possible village members, you'll place their names on the chart accordingly.

"If you're not sure who to incorporate into your chart, think about all the people who are affected by your work, who have influence on it or power over it, or who have an interest in its successful or unsuccessful conclusion. This might include customers, senior executives, shareholders, suppliers, your boss, your coworkers, your family, your divisional team members, and even people in your community.

"Remember, while your village may include individuals from both inside and outside your organization, it will only be made up of people with whom you are able to actually communicate. Someone who barely knows you—either at work or outside the office—is unlikely to have a vested interest in your success or lack thereof.

"Mathew, why don't you have a crack at explaining the top right quadrant," the PIE Guy finished.

Mathew stood and took the floor. "The individuals who land in the first quadrant have a high vested interest in your success. These are people who like you as a person and who are close to you and to the work you currently perform or the benefits of the work you perform."

"That is exactly how I would have described it," the PIE Guy said. "Now, Toni, how about describing the villagers in the second and third quadrants?"

"The individuals positioned in the second quadrant [upper left] like you but they have a low vested interest in the work you perform at present," Toni mused. "The individuals you have placed in the third quadrant [lower right] are indifferent about you or don't really like you but they have a high vested interest in your work."

"You're right on the money, Toni," agreed the PIE Guy. "The only thing I would add is that people in the upper left quadrant are most likely to give you honest feedback about your ideas, performance, and areas for improvement, whereas people in the lower right will provide honest feedback about your leadership or your performance. Although it may come across as a bit harsh or even as a personal attack, their insight is invaluable when determining ways to be a more likeable leader or professional.

"Okay, Clare, tell us about the people in the last quadrant," the PIE Guy said.

"I don't think I like those people," said Clare. "They probably don't like you or your work."

"You're right," the PIE Guy stated. "They may not be very friendly, but it's best to understand who these people are and to keep them on your radar. You don't need to spend too much time on them unless they are critical to your future success.

"Make a list of the people you've noted in quadrants one through three. These are your village members," he concluded. "I'll give you all a few moments to work on this exercise in your notebooks. I need to eat my lunch."

The PIE Guy took a hearty bite out of a turkey club and chewed with great gusto as the group scribbled away. By the time he had finished his sandwich and had deposited his trash in the nearby wastebasket, most appeared ready to continue the lesson.

"Let's talk about your villages," he said. "Who wants to start?"

"I'll start," said Clare. "I think you are all in my village. I'm getting valuable ideas from all of you—not just from the PIE Guy —and the group benefits from using my café as a place to meet and talk. We're here for each other."

"Super! And who else is part of your village?" the PIE Guy prodded.

"The people who work for me," she responded.

"And how do you benefit from that relationship? What benefits do they get?" he asked.

"Well, they get a job and I get people to help with the work," she replied. "But I know it can be more than that. While I want my business to be successful, I also want the people who work for me to be successful. So maybe I need to make more of an effort to understand what they need and how I can set them up for success in future roles. If the word gets out that Café Creo Prosperitas is a great place to work, it will be easier to hire new staff. Plus, if I'm making the training and development of my team a priority, I think I'll have fewer problems with turnover."

"Excellent," said the PIE Guy. "Who do you have in your village, Stuart?"

"A couple of my peers. I have good conversations with them and we share some personal professional things, if you know what I mean. There are a few friends in the neighborhood that talk about work and often one person will introduce an issue and the rest of us chime in with solutions. They'd be part of my village," Stuart said thoughtfully.

"My village also includes a few people from my Toastmasters group, and there's a non-profit organization that I support by helping with some fundraising. The leaders and I generally have good conversations about this type of thing," he concluded.

"Fabulous!" the PIE Guy asserted. "And Mathew, what have you gifted or given your village?"

"I'm not sure," Mathew replied. "My network is pretty large, but I'm not sure about my village. My network consists of all the people I've sold financial services to in the past, and there have been a lot of them. But I guess I haven't really tapped into those people for anything other than sales, nor have I tried to give them anything other than the services the company provides in return."

"Because you have to know a lot about someone's life to guide them to financial security, you've probably built pretty strong relationships with some of your clients. Can you include any of them in your village? How about your colleagues?" the PIE Guy prodded.

Thinking further Mathew stated, "There are a few clients I have a more meaningful relationship with. They have taken a personal interest in me and we know each other's families. But my colleagues seem more interested in moaning and complaining about everything they think is wrong with their jobs than doing anything to fix what they see as problems. When I suggest possible solutions, they rarely acknowledge my input. And they definitely don't implement it."

"Hmm," the PIE Guy mused, "your colleagues definitely don't sound like village members. However, you may be able to convert some of them into valuable allies if you get to know them better. You have to learn what is important to them. This will later allow you to align your thoughts, actions, growth, and development with theirs."

"You mean I need to suck up to people in order to progress?" Mathew interjected disdainfully.

Success requires alignment of your village support.

"Absolutely not!" the PIE Guy exclaimed. "This is about something bigger than our own ego or others' egos. This is about alignment, not caving in or pandering. Alignment involves creating momentum in a positive way by helping others while helping yourself."

"Charles, let's talk about your company's manufacturing expansion plans and how they fit with your village. What happens to them if you proceed?" the PIE Guy asked.

"I have both internal and external villagers. If we expand production overseas to sell our bicycles to a wider market, both groups of villagers would have to deal with some changes. Those changes might be especially dramatic for my immediate team and my family, as I'd have less time for them while focusing on a larger global business," Charles responded.

"I want to do what's right for the people who have helped build this business. And I want to do what's right for my family. They understand that I sometimes need to be away for business, but neither my wife nor my kids would be happy to have me out of the country for extended periods," Charles continued.

"And then there's the company's external village: suppliers, customers, the race team, etc. They want more access to our products, but I'm not certain they're willing to continue paying premium prices for these bikes. Maybe there are other options I can explore that will still help us grow, but will also satisfy my villagers," he pondered. "Maybe I can talk to my team about different strategies that will increase revenue and decrease the cost base without changing our image."

"That sounds like a wise course of action, linked to your thoughts on becoming a better leader," said the PIE Guy. "What are your thoughts about your village, Toni?"

"My village understands my need for world domination," she said with a laugh. "But seriously, I've already made a pretty good start building mutually beneficial relationships with other individuals and companies that share similar goals and values. I'm sure I can make a few improvements, but I think my village is well in hand."

"Awesome," the PIE Guy said. "How about you, Nimmi? Do you have a handle on your villagers?"

"These discussions are certainly helping me work toward a better understanding of villagers," Nimmi replied. "I believe I have internal and external villagers, and I now know my internal villagers include my core staff. While I can't pay them the kind of money they'd get in the for-profit sector, I am able to give my staff opportunities to do things that only senior officers in a profit-based company get to do. If I can help them recognize the value of this, it will be easier to retain my staff. This is as close as I can get to a reciprocal investment with my village."

"Excellent, and what about your external villagers?" the PIE Guy inquired.

"My sponsors, and perhaps the volunteers, are external members of my village," she stated. "I know they believe in our cause because I've taken the time to get to know them and build relationships with them individually. However, I think I could do a better job of bringing them together to create something even bigger. I need to learn how to leverage all the great connections I have."

"That's a good point," said the PIE Guy. "It's also one we're going to be touching on in our next session. Leveraging connections can help us achieve more with the little time we have in our working life."

As he stood and stretched he said, "Nimmi, would you recap today's session?"

Our success is dependent upon others.

Surround yourself with great people.

Nimmi obliged. "To recap today's discussion, our success is dependent on others. We can only do so much on our own. Whether we like it or not, we need to rely on others to help. The best way to get that help is to give help. Helping others to succeed will help us to find greater success."

Mathew added, "In a way, our village is kind of like a bank account. You can't always make withdrawals. You need to make deposits into your village, and you do so by setting other people up for success."

"Excellent, Mathew. I like the bank account metaphor," said the PIE Guy. "Does anyone have anything else to add?"

Toni piped up, "I thought it was an interesting concept to map people using the quadrants. It helped me think about what type of help people could offer."

"I couldn't agree more," stated the PIE Guy. "It helps us to appreciate relationships more, and to value the input of those that we wouldn't normally expect to develop a relationship with and a few where we wouldn't expect to extract any value.

"I know you all have businesses to run and things to do, so let's call it quits for now and meet back here on Thursday night after Clare has closed the café for the evening."

CHAPTER 6

BUILDING YOUR SUCCESS PIE

"One of the most courageous things you can do is
identify yourself, know who you are,
what you believe in and where you want to go."

Sheila Murray Bethel

The sun disappeared behind the mountains, leaving gold-gilded clouds in its wake. As the first stars began to appear in the night sky, the windows of Café Creo Prosperitas glowed welcomingly. Though the last customer had left long ago, the café was not empty. The members of the PIE Guy's personal development group bustled about, pointing at flipcharts stuck to the walls, scribbling in notebooks, and discussing their Success PIEs with the people around them.

"Everyone, gather around," the PIE Guy called out, motioning the group toward their usual table in the corner. "It's time to talk about conversations. There are actually two types, and I often refer to them as the 'Donut of Life' because in the old days many a conversation here in the States took place over a donut and a cup of coffee. I'm talking really black and bitter coffee, not the high quality ristretto-based coffees of today. The kind of coffee that would 'put hair on your chest,' as they used to say.

"But I digress. Only Clare is likely to appreciate a chat about the nectar of the business world. Where was I prior to that drooling and tantalizing trip down memory lane?" he asked himself, scratching his head.

"Oh yes, the Donut of Life. There are only two types of conversations: interesting conversations and productive conversations. That's not to say that productive conversations can't be productive and interesting conversations, but interesting conversations are rarely productive conversations.

"Interesting conversations are those conversations about things that we have little control over, like an Indian cricket match or a European football game, or what is happening with Chinese interest rates or their impact on the value of the dollar or euro. These are only interesting from a personal perspective. There is little we can do to influence the outcome—unless you are the Chairman of the Federal Reserve or financial head of your country.

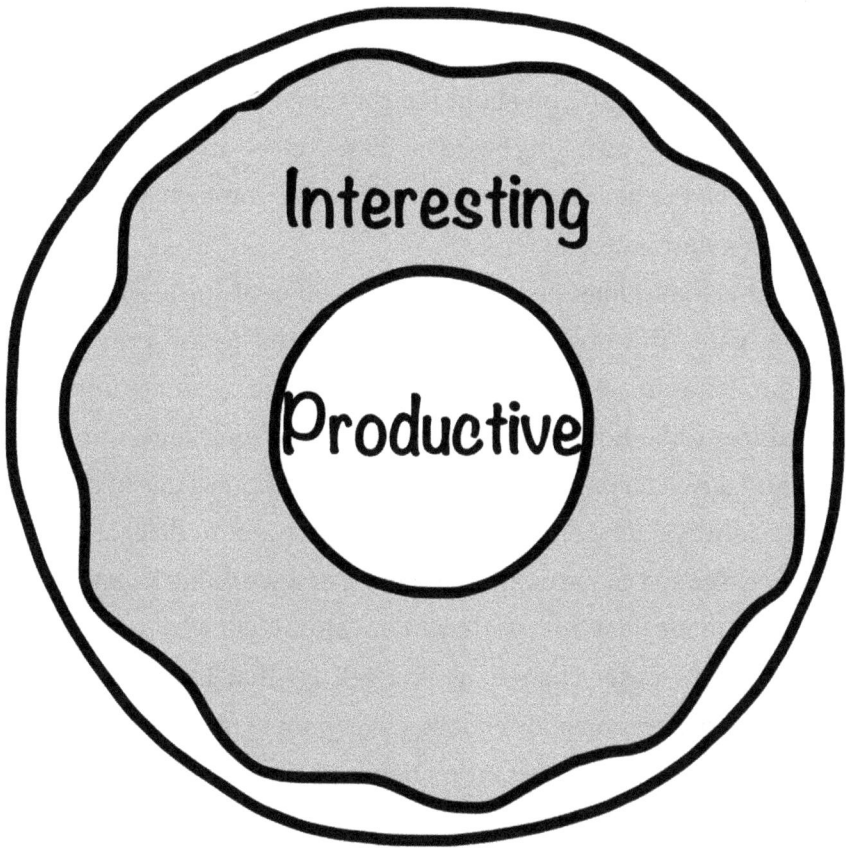

Interesting

Productive

"Productive conversations, on the other hand, are chats where we can make a difference because we are in control of the outcome.

"We've had really great productive conversations during our time as a group. I thank you for speaking honestly and openly. What matters most for me, at this point, is we've learned what resonates with each of you. What are you going to do differently based on the discussions we've had? This is where we convert those productive conversations into action. Remember, it is action, not intention, that drives us toward our goals.

"I'd love to hear three things from each of you," he continued. "What resonates with you about the conversations we've had so far? What actions are you taking based on these conversations? And finally, what will be the benefits of those actions once you have taken them? Clare, let's start with you."

"I've actually intended to do things different for a while now," Clare began. "But now that I've been exposed to the principles of PIE, I'm going to act on those intentions. I'm going to get important procedures—like how to open the café in the morning—out of my head and down on paper so that my staff can take on some of the tasks that I've always done on my own. I want to be able to delegate that to someone else so I can actually enjoy more of a work-life balance.

"And that's just for starters. I've also identified other small steps—or first order change, as you call it—that I can take. These include giving responsibility for stockkeeping to my best barista. I'm going to offer her the assistant manager position, which I think will engage her and keep her around.

"I'm also going to introduce another signature muffin. That will include exploring what will make my customers really happy. I'm even going to introduce sales bonuses for my staff. They'll learn new skills in order to better sell our products, and that will make them— and the café—more successful.

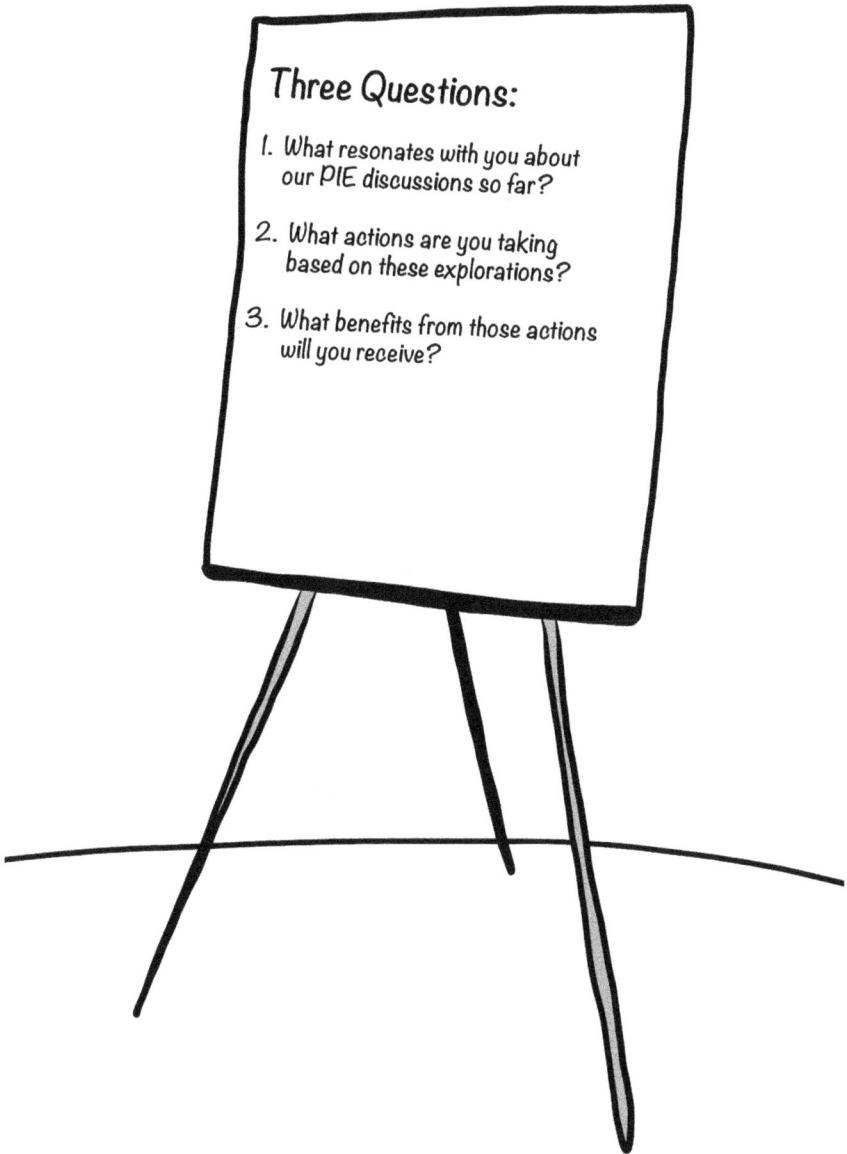

Three Questions:

1. What resonates with you about our PIE discussions so far?

2. What actions are you taking based on these explorations?

3. What benefits from those actions will you receive?

"These are the actions I'm doing to achieve better results, and they'll all have a dramatic impact on my life and the lives of my staff. I'll be less grumpy in the morning, and they'll be more engaged in their jobs and feel like they're really part of the company. I think that's going to go pretty far in reducing staff turnover," Clare concluded.

"I'm glad to see you focusing on the benefits," the PIE Guy interjected. "But when are you going to do these things?"

"I've already begun!" Clare exclaimed with pride. "Rebecca jumped at the opportunity to be assistant manager, keep the stock records, and open the café three mornings a week. The remaining items are on my calendar, and I've carved out time when I know business is slow to make progress in each area. I know it's not going to be easy, but I'm more committed than ever to make something good into something even better."

"Why am I not surprised?" the PIE Guy asked with a smile. "What about you, Stuart?"

"It's amazing how much Clare and I have in common, given that we are in totally different industries," Stuart said. "I'm also interested in a better work-life balance, because right now I work nonstop throughout the week, which isn't great for my relationship. I have a serious girlfriend, and we've talked about marriage, but she really only gets quality time with me on the weekends. So building a Success PIE is as important for my relationship as it is for my career.

"I suppose that realization is what has resonated with me the most. Like Clare, I've thought about making changes for a long time, especially after not having the same sense of enjoyment since taking on this new role and team. Just getting the work done has always taken precedence and provided results. I've never found myself with the need to make changes in the way I managed. For this reason, scheduling time to think about necessary changes to become a better leader is going to be a really important aspect of my Success PIE," he concluded.

The PIE Guy quickly interjected, "Just make sure you're not spending too much time thinking and too little time taking action. The real danger in the thinking stage of your Success PIE is staying in intention. Some people call it the 'paralysis of analysis.' It's basically too much thinking and not enough action or progress on the important things.

"Intention, or telling yourself—or others—*what* you are going to do, is easy and requires no effort, but actual change requires Effort. If it didn't, I would become the 'Pi' Guy and start giving lectures in mathematics instead of personal development," he said with a smile. "Are all of these things that you can do in the near future able to be done without a huge amount of effort?"

"I guess I might be a step behind Clare because I'm still thinking about what changes to make," Stuart acknowledged. "But I sure don't want to get caught in the 'intention trap.' So off the top of my head, I think I can manage one change in the next two weeks or so. I'll ask my team about ideas to create a bit of fun during the next off-site regional meeting.

"A big part of what I need to do with my Success PIE involves including my village. I know many people in different circles that have achieved success in collaborating, leading, developing teams, engaging staff, and creating diverse teams that perform exceptionally well. I need to leverage those relationships to learn more through their experiences. In the past, my focus has been on learning through workshops, especially early on when I needed to improve my technical skills and customer service. The facilitators in those workshops told me I asked great questions and listened to truly understand the content. What I've learned here is that there are multiple ways to learn, in workshops *and* through my village. I need to develop the ability to share with others after the workshops and ask more in-depth questions about how people implement change. Part of my effort is going to be opening up and having productive conversations that matter instead of only interesting conversations," Stuart finished.

"It sounds like the facilitators you've mentioned are giving you insight into why your customers like you and have an image of you that surpasses your team's perception of you. Your presence here would indicate that you are serious about your development and about becoming a more successful leader. Perhaps one of your peers or people in one of the circles you've mentioned could provide you with the support you need to keep you on track with your progress," the PIE Guy pointed out while Stuart was busy making notes in his journal.

"Mathew, I must say I'm impressed," the PIE Guy continued, turning to the finance pro who was usually dressed impeccably. "You're not wearing a three-piece suit today. You really are serious about implementing your Success PIE."

"I guess there are no worries about me stalling at intent!" Mathew declared. "But joking aside, I'm a little concerned about making changes to the way I've been doing things. My family is really important to me, and there's a lot riding on my success. If I

Keep Your PIE Fresh

were to lose some of my commissions—or even worse, lose my job entirely—I don't know what we'd do!"

"That sounds like a lot of pressure," the PIE Guy said soothingly. "Tell me a bit more about your relationship with your wife. I'm sure she wants you to be happy as well as successful."

"Of course," Mathew replied. "We've always worked together so

Past successes don't guarantee future success.

we could both be as happy as possible. We even put together a family game plan when we got married. We talked about what we wanted for our personal lives and our careers. We decided who would work and who would take primary responsibility for raising the family. Because my wife wanted to study more, it made sense for her to stay home with our children. I have better earning potential—at least until my wife finishes her advanced degree.

"That's one of the reasons I've been afraid to change. There's a lot at stake if I fail. What I've been doing seems to be working—even if I haven't advanced any further—so I've just kept doing it," he said with a sigh, "but I haven't received the promotion I thought I deserved."

"Then it's time for a reality check!" the PIE Guy proclaimed. "We can all use the occasional reminder that what made us successful in the past isn't always what is going to make us successful in the future. As we advance through different stages of life, things change.

"I know many couples who have had the same conversation that you've had about creating a family game plan. More and more, I am seeing this conversation end up with roles reversed and the husband staying at home to be the primary caregiver for the children. Regardless of what ends up working for you, the important thing is that you are having real conversations that matter with your wife. These are productive conversations and they demonstrate the health and maturity of your relationship.

"I understand the risk element, and this is where it's important to look at the changes that are happening around you. Part of Preparedness that we discussed earlier this week looked at areas we could explore to identify gaps that we need to bridge with learning and development. You've identified another important area to explore: your environment. You have to think about what you need to do to stay current with your peers and what you can do to take advantage of the experience you have. The worst thing that could happen is that by not changing and relying on your successes of the past, your peers, who are changing, end up getting better results and passing you in performance," he concluded.

"That's exactly what has been happening to me," Mathew said. "The way you look at success from so many different angles is very impressive...and how you've created an easy-to-understand journey is, well, genius!"

"Why, thanks. All this is much easier from an outsider's perspective," said the PIE Guy. "But how is PIE going to help you?"

"In order to advance in my career, I'm going to have to change from an individual contributor into a leader—someone who understands stakeholders, management, leading teams, and collaboration," Mathew replied.

"Moving from an individual contributor to a leader sounds like a pretty big change," said the PIE Guy. "Have you broken this into smaller steps?"

"I believe I have," Mathew continued. "Over the next six months, I'm going to look at people one or two levels above me and figure out what they are doing differently that has allowed them to achieve their results. Part of this Preparedness step involves getting to know a few of these individuals better and having real conversations with them.

"As far as the 'I' in PIE, I know my outward image is formal because I am always dressed in a three-piece suit, but through others in these sessions, I've discovered that my appearance may make people uncomfortable and affect the depth of conversations I am able to achieve. So, if changing the way I dress allows me to have better conversations with people because they feel more comfortable, well, that's an easy change to make. Thanks for that lesson, Stuart.

"So the Effort I am going to take will revolve around these things. I will make better connections with people by changing the way that I dress, helping them feel more relaxed. I will engage people in conversations about non-work related topics to build stronger relationships with more depth. And I'll look for a mentor in my organization—someone who does the job that I would like to do. He or she can help me understand how to lead people and get results through others," Mathew finished.

"Your forward planning sounds good and your goals realistic," the PIE Guy affirmed. "What are you going to do first?"

"I think I need to start by securing additional support. Some of the changes are a bit daunting," Mathew admitted. "But I'm beginning to feel like a champion!"

"Great news, Mathew! I like the mentoring idea. Perhaps supplement that with support from a coach, as they both offer complementary, yet different, perspectives," said the PIE Guy.

"That's a good idea," Mathew agreed.

"Wonderful. Over to you, Charles," the PIE Guy said.

"I helped start this company back in the days of steel-framed mountain bikes," Charles said. "The company's first office was actually in my garage. As a result, I'm very close to the business, perhaps even too close. In the past, I had the ability to hover at the 10,000-foot level and look at the big picture as well as dive into the details with great confidence that I'm going to be right.

"So the things that have most resonated with me are the ideas of success being linked to my village and that past success isn't a guarantee of future success. We surrounded ourselves with great people who have helped build this company, but I haven't been a great leader in my area who engages people in building future

strategies. I've just asked them to carry out my vision rather than taking ownership of a vision we've created together.

"I need to look at engaging people and recognizing their ideas for the future of this organization as we consider adjustments to shifts in the industry," Charles finished.

"What are the specific things you need to do differently to accomplish this?" the PIE Guy asked.

"I want to lead, inspire, and motivate my team, and tap into their knowledge instead of just driving my ideas," Charles replied. "I'll use 360 feedback to find out what my team needs from me as a leader. I'll also start to trust the talented, knowledgeable, and clever people I have working for me to worry about the details. This will include involving my senior leadership team in strategy and vision building for the future. My senior leadership team, aka SLT, can help with research and staying current with changes in the industry.

"I'm also going to share what I've learned about PIE with my SLT to help them be better leaders in their own right. I want to inspire them to take more ownership rather than managing them," Charles concluded.

"This is great, Charles," the PIE Guy said. "Not all the people I work with take things onboard and then say, 'What's good for me must be good for my team as well.' I applaud your efforts in teaching what you have learned here to your team and passing the knowledge along. How long will it take you to implement your Success PIE?"

"There's a lot of work that needs to be done, but I don't think it will take long to implement my PIE. I'm putting together my agenda for change to implement the week I return to Scotland," Charles replied. "But I imagine it's going to take a long time to perfect it."

"Minor correction there, Charles. PIE is about progress, not perfection," said the PIE Guy with a laugh. "What are your thoughts on all of this, Toni?"

"I've always been driven and I always get results, so effort isn't a problem for me," Toni began.

"Ah, but Effort isn't just about your business results," the PIE Guy interrupted. "Effort is linked to PIE and your personal development. Building your Success PIE is a holistic look at each component of PIE and thinking through the steps needed to make the change. In this instance, you identified that by focusing on your Image. You could improve your ability to engage your team with your vision. Once a change is identified, it will enable you to be more successful. Effort means scheduling time to focus on the required change, or using your words, you can apply your 'drive to get a result' by making the change a reality."

"Thanks for that reminder," said Toni. "So in light of what you've said, what really resonates with me is the idea that PIE will work for me, and it's a process that's easy to comprehend and apply in my busy life. I'm focusing on leadership for my personal development.

"I'm going to start by making a better effort to lead my team and to leverage and engage the younger people in my extended team. They are talented resources that are currently untapped and we could potentially lose them. This will require slowing down and listening more, and having two-way engaging conversations instead of directive monologues. As I get to know more about them personally, I think it will build trust and respect.

"I also need to reevaluate my senior leadership team. I brought people into the team who were just like me, so we don't have the best mix. We all tend to have aggressive conversations because everyone is so driven and has a type A personality, just like me. Fixing this may require restructuring my organizational chart for better balance," Toni said.

"How does this tie into your Success PIE?" the PIE Guy said encouragingly.

"Preparedness for me means recognizing the need to change, and there are plenty of datapoints supporting my need to improve my leadership capabilities. The end result will be a positive impact on others. I can play to my strengths as someone who gets results, while recognizing my limitations and leveraging someone else who can help rally the people and get them motivated," she continued. "I'll work with my leadership team to determine what we need to do slightly differently to get better results. We can also work together to determine what changes we can make to ensure significant growth over the next two years and what organizational structure will be required to achieve that vision. That's the Preparedness part.

"I need to enhance my Image as a senior executive as well. I need to better understand others' strengths, and change behaviors to engage them according to their strengths. I need to explore how I use my leadership skills to build a better brand internally and reap the rewards of an engaged workforce.

"Finally, I'll ask them for assistance with Effort. Together, we'll determine how to prioritize the changes required and to check the progress we are making. We will figure out who can help us, how to share our plan, and how often we need to talk to them about it," she finished, slightly out of breath.

"Clearly you have been leveraging the fast processing power of that brain of yours," the PIE Guy chuckled. "This is great. Once the concept of PIE is grasped, it's easy to apply. One final question: Why do this? What are the benefits?"

"One, leverage people's talents. Two, engage their minds. Three, free up time for me to think more widely about vision and strategy. And four, build greater team success using this simple model. No offense intended, PIE Guy," Toni stated succinctly.

"None taken," the PIE Guy replied. "You've actually mentioned an important point. It's essential to use simple models that work. Complexity will creep in. If we start with complex models, complexity is already there. It makes implementing change or transformations that much more challenging and prone to failure."

"Thanks, Toni." The PIE Guy turned to Nimmi. "How about you?"

"What resonates for me is the idea of continuing to do what I do well while making personal and organizational changes to improve the things I could do better," said Nimmi. "For example, I'm a decent leader, but I could be better. One of the ways I can improve is to transfer my skills from one area to another, such as taking what I've learned from speaking with donors and using it to enhance the retention of my volunteers.

"We are always talking to donors about the ways their contributions benefit the people our organization helps. Our volunteers believe in the cause and generously donate their time to help, but I haven't talked to my volunteers about how giving us their time can actually be a benefit to them as well. They're learning valuable skills. They're gaining experience that is difficult to find in the for-profit world unless you're an executive.

"I'm pretty overwhelmed at the moment, so my vision is really still in my head. But it's clear as to what needs to be done. I'm really excited about the future," Nimmi finished.

"Clearly you are a great thinker," said the PIE Guy. "But I'd like to suggest that you make the time to write your ideas down now. Not only is it a very cathartic exercise, but it's also an important step in clarifying what you want to achieve.

"We speak at 200 plus words per minute—even more if we have a second cup of Clare's delicious coffee—but when we write our thoughts down on paper or enter them in a digital format, it forces us to slow down and think. Also, clarity comes from writing down and sharing with others. It's an important step in building a vision that others can understand before you start to implement change," he stated.

Clarity comes from writing your ideas down and sharing them with others.

"This is very similar to the feedback I get on a regular basis," Nimmi said with a sigh. "People are always telling me that I have too much going on in my head. Perhaps, as you suggest, writing things down will help."

"It really is great feedback," said the PIE Guy. "But don't just write down your thoughts, share them as well! Having your Success PIE written down but not shared is not much better than having it only in your head."

"I think I'm going to need help with this, it's a bit overwhelming. I could use some examples," Nimmi said.

"I'd be happy to work with you individually outside of this meeting. The others have been writing in their journals every day about things they have learned in our sessions. You did miss a few key sessions because of your schedule," the PIE Guy responded. "Those sessions may have helped add clarity by listening to others share their experiences and thoughts. We have a tremendous ability to learn from others. It's actually one of the reasons I run group coaching sessions. Learning through others' experiences and mistakes is less costly and helps accelerate our own learning."

"I feel my hand was just slapped in the nicest possible way," Nimmi said with a shy smile. "But you are right. I missed some sessions because I prioritized things above and beyond my own development and devalued the importance of what you've put together. I've scheduled a block of time in my weekly diary to devote to my Success PIE. It's strange, I've been very successful in building this organization, but until now, I've not realized there was still room for personal growth. I actually thought about moving on to another organization to grow and apply what I've learned."

"Sorry about the hand slap," said the PIE Guy with a grin. "Sometimes when learning programs are designed, the journey is just as important as the destination.

"Thinking about that comment you made about personal growth and changing organizations, there are so many opportunities to grow and develop. It doesn't really matter which organization employs you. It's more about your mindset and how you look at improving your work performance," the PIE Guy concluded.

"Today's focus was building your Success PIE—what needs to be accomplished, the reasons why this is important, and when you'll begin," the PIE Guy said reassuringly. "Who would like to share what resonated for you?"

Mathew quickly piped up. "It's not always easy to share this type of information with people inside the company, but sharing and learning from others in this group has given me insight well beyond my own thinking. The other thing that resonates for me is finding a few people inside the company and taking them on my journey of PIE, as you have done with us," said Mathew.

"It certainly helps people to align with you if they understand what is behind your change. Then they're able to more easily recognize your efforts," explained the PIE Guy.

Nimmi added, "When it comes to my development, I am the only one that can make things happen, and it's action, not intention, that leads to progress. I need to take control of my development by having productive *and* interesting conversations. This will be the best way to build a series of Success PIEs," beamed Nimmi.

People will judge you by your actions, not your intentions.

"Precisely! Once you've experienced the sequence and built your first Success PIE, it's much easier to replicate," explained the PIE Guy. "Well, that's it for now. Because today is a long session, let's take a break and refill our cups before we explore expediting our success by sharing it with key people, because success doesn't happen in a vacuum."

CHAPTER 7

SHARING YOUR SUCCESS PIE

"The stories we tell literally make the world. If you want to change the world, you need to change your story.

Michael Margolis

After a short break to refuel on coffee and leftover muffins, the PIE Guy and his personal development group returned to their favorite table in the warmly lit corner of Café Creo Prosperitas.

"Have you ever received an email and felt the sender wasn't really thinking about what you needed to know or hear?" the PIE Guy began. "Or maybe you've attended a corporate presentation that simply left you cold. Some organizations have fantastic communication strategies and dedicated people to ensure that the right messages go to the right people at the right time. What we need to do is emulate, in a small way, what organizations do to ensure we understand our audience, our village, and their needs. We want to bring them in at the right time when we have something to share that may be useful for them or help them in some way.

"Whether you need to communicate general day-to-day information or convey big news about major changes, the best conversations start with your village members in mind. So, the first step is to put yourself in their shoes. What do they know, need to know, and want to hear? What's their preferred way of receiving information? What will stop them from listening to what you have to say? And how will you know that they have understood your message?" he asked.

Toni chimed in, "It's like what I was saying about my stakeholders earlier. I need to ensure I speak their language to really connect with them, but you're taking this a step beyond by saying we don't discuss everything with everyone. Right?"

"Brilliant, Toni. This PIE stuff isn't complicated, and even better, it's based on many things we currently do in our day jobs," the PIE

Guy responded. "Let's dive into what you can do to have a great conversation with your village and ensure they hear the message you want to deliver," he said as the group turned to fresh pages in their notebooks.

Building success is an iterative process.

"Like we're doing tonight, it's always nice to share PIE over a cup of coffee," he explained. "Creating the right environment to share your Success PIE with your village is an important aspect of generating great conversations. It is one thing to understand what you need to do to achieve greater success, but it's another thing to be able to articulate that need in such a way that you inspire others to get involved.

"The best way to do this is to create a compelling vision that outlines three things that your audience can immediately understand. This includes why you're sharing, what the benefits are, and your actual vision. There's no need to go into megadetail unless a village member asks for it. When that happens, it's a bonus because you'll realize you have a village member who really cares.

"As Simon Sinek helped us understand through his *Golden Circles*, most people share what they do for a living but not *why* they do it. This is unfortunate, because it inhibits the formation of a deep personal connection. When you make that personal connection—by being open and approachable so that the right villagers want to know more about you—you'll be better able to more readily engage them in your vision. This vision is less about the details of what you want to do and more about how it ties into something bigger, something that your village members may want to achieve as well," he concluded.

"In light of this," the PIE Guy said, turning to Toni, "how are you going to communicate your message with your village once you're back to the daily grind?"

"Well, I've got a network of hundreds," Toni replied, "so I'm going to use social media to communicate with them. This will require using Twitter and LinkedIn and…"

The PIE Guy gently interrupted, "Sounds like you may be marketing your company instead of talking to your village about how you are going to develop personally to get better results. I was talking about managing your relationship with your village of eight to twelve people with whom you have a mutually supportive relationship.

"When we focus on the eight to twelve people in our village, we are sharing information to seek support, and to help others. We're telling them about what's working for us—information, tools, conversations, tips, and techniques—so they may be able to use this themselves or pass it on to other people. We are sharing our success and our failures to ensure that our villagers can learn vicariously from our successes as well as from our mistakes. It's the kind of information you may not want your entire network to have—especially if that network includes any competitors.

"While there's no right or wrong size for a village, the members are typically people we know very well. If you know 50 people very well, you may choose to have 50 people in your village. But maybe you only know eight people really well—so well that you know their spouses, and children's names, and their favorite family vacation spots. In that case, you'd have eight people in your village," he finished.

"I actually know about 100 people that well," Toni stated. "Would you like me to list them for you?" she asked cheekily.

"Impressive, but that's not necessary," said the PIE Guy. "If that's the case, then for you, one of the key things to think through is how to efficiently and productively communicate with a village of this size. Because Success PIEs are always changing, you're going to need to have a lot of conversations."

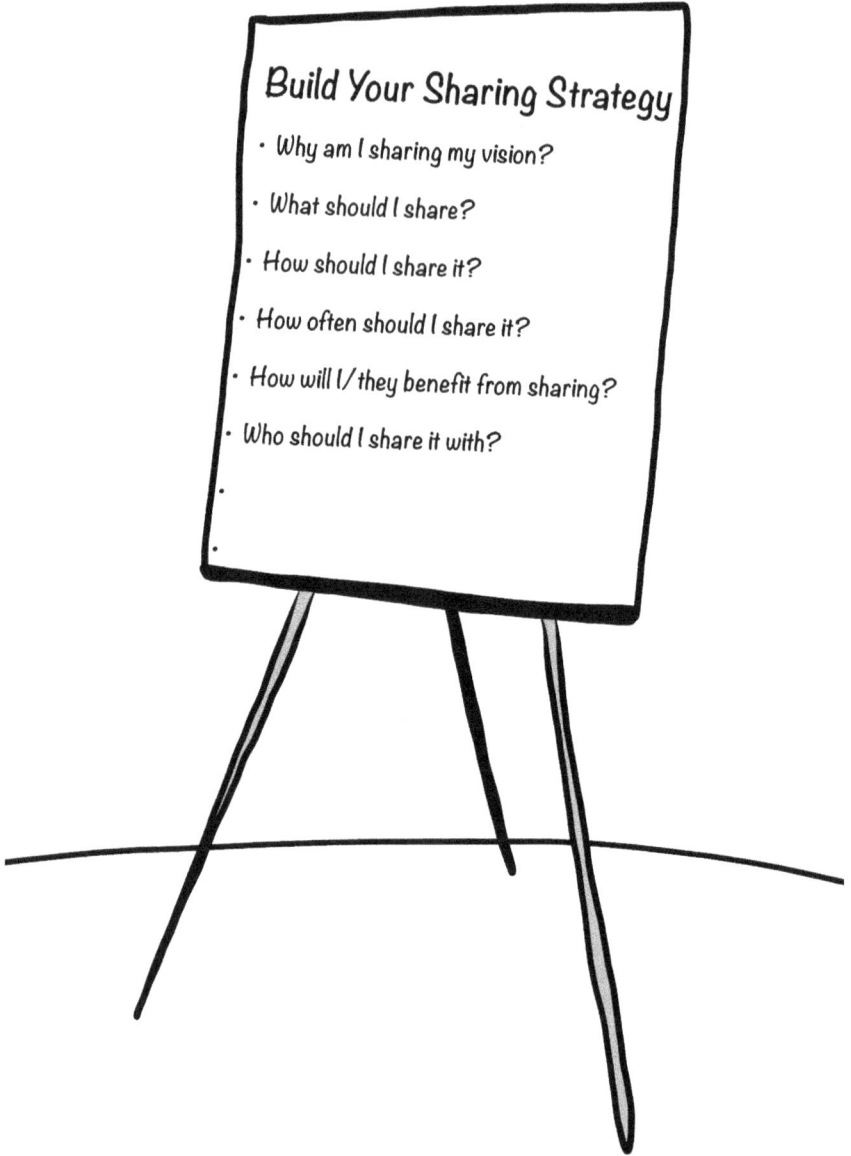

Build Your Sharing Strategy

- Why am I sharing my vision?
- What should I share?
- How should I share it?
- How often should I share it?
- How will I/they benefit from sharing?
- Who should I share it with?
-
-

"Good point," Toni said thoughtfully. "I don't have time to nurture relationships with 100 people. I think I'll start with the 30 or so people in my office. I can schedule a 'lunch and learn' and tell them about my vision, which is an important component of my Success PIE. I can reach out to them again through social media and maybe have a few of the more interested ones over to my house for coffee and further discussion.

"If I can break my village down into groups based on their level of interest, I can spend more time communicating with the ones who are most interested, and then figure out an efficient way to share the basics with the other groups in order to maximize the results," she concluded, smiling with satisfaction.

"Perfect!" the PIE Guy exclaimed. "You're really getting this now. How will you share this with your village, Clare?"

"Unlike Toni, my village is very small," Clare replied. "It's mostly made up of the obvious ones—my staff, and a few friends who have supported me from the beginning with financial backing for the café. But there's another group of people I need to include in my village, my family. I need to include them so they know that not only am I trying to build a successful business, but that they should also expect changes in the near future and will have a mother and wife who's around more. For the former groups, I think casual, informal chats will probably be enough to communicate my Success PIE. However, for my family I need to do something special. Perhaps I could arrange a long weekend away and talk to them."

"I really like how you've included your family into your village!" the PIE Guy exclaimed enthusiastically. "Having conversations with family helps to ensure that there is alignment and support for both Success PIE equations: work and home. I've talked with people that have had great results by discussing their Success PIE with their children. It has strengthened their relationships with their children, and helped their kids to understand some of the challenges adults face. Of course this depends on the age of the children, but it's surprising how messages can be adapted so even the very young can understand. These conversations change over time, and even if you don't have children, success can be enhanced if open conversations with a spouse or partner explore Success PIE options and the support required for various paths."

> Villagers have a vested interest in you and in your success.

Claire continued, "My husband has been instrumental in helping me achieve the results in the café. However, I'm not sure I've done the best job at managing his or the children's expectations. There are a few other people I need to include in my village—a few who I don't know quite as well yet have helped support my initial interest in setting up the café and putting together my business plan for a commercial loan. I will need to use a more formal method to share my PIE with them.

"I was thinking about throwing a small private party for these people to both celebrate the success I've had so far and to show my appreciation for the support they gave me five years ago. I want them to know that I value the fact that they believed in me and supported me with their knowledge or finances, and helped me realize a dream.

"Before I do that, however, I want to spend a little more time creating a vision for what the future holds for Café Creo Prosperitas. I can then include that vision when communicating with my village," she concluded.

"Bravo!" said the PIE Guy, clapping enthusiastically before turning to the next professional at the table. "Stuart, tell us how you'll share your Success PIE with your village."

"My village is growing, especially since taking on this new role," Stuart began. "I know there are members of my circles that I haven't tapped into enough. I want to get to know a few more people in these groups better and eventually include some of them at the core of my village."

"That sounds like a good way to strengthen your village," the PIE Guy said. "So how will you share your Success PIE at this point?"

"First off, I'm not going to call it a Success PIE," Stuart responded with a laugh. "If I talk to the people in my village that way, they're going to have a go at me—that's Aussie-speak for 'give me a hard time.' So I'm just going to say I am working on my leadership capabilities, work-life balance, and my personal vision, and I'll weave it into a few stories shared over a beer and a few prawns on the barbie during a weekend."

"Actually, you've hit on something very important," the PIE Guy said. "Before history was written, our ancient ancestors used to tell stories around a fire to pass knowledge on, or perhaps even have a laugh or two. Storytelling has been making its way back into the corporate sector over the last several years, and it is an effective medium for driving change. Telling stories helps people relate to what you are sharing by putting it into words and mental images that resonate with them. It works amazingly well!"

"I must be a master then," Stuart said, "because I use storytelling with my team to help them help customers and to visualize what their finished project will look like."

"I am sure you are a master at many things you don't even realize," the PIE Guy said with a smile.

"What Stuart has said really resonates with me," Mathew interjected. "I've been in sales for donkey's years—how's that for a British expression—and I've just realized one of the greatest tools in my sales bag is my ability to talk through different scenarios. I guess what I've actually been doing is storytelling, and you've helped me rethink how to communicate more effectively with my village.

"Right now, my village includes my family and only a few people in the company. Like we've discussed before, I want to expand my village. But first, I need to really think through what's in it for them. There's so much to do. Sometimes I worry that it's too much, especially when I need to keep up with my job and spend time with my family at home," he finished with a sigh.

"I've seen this countless times before, Mathew," the PIE Guy said. "It does seem insurmountable at times, especially when we think about all the complexities of what needs to be accomplished in life. Perhaps you are thinking too much about second order change, where a radical rethink is needed to achieve greater results. You might feel better about the time required if you focus on one thing you would like to achieve that's manageable and a quick win. That will help you learn the process of PIE and how to replicate it in the future."

"What is it you always say…?" Mathew interjected. "'Simple works.'"

"That's right," the PIE Guy replied. "'Simple works' is one of my mantras. Complexity is often present in our day jobs, so if we want to develop and grow, the last thing we need is a complex personal development model to follow. It might help you to think about high level questions," he said, walking to the flipchart and turning to a page with questions prewritten on it.

"Actually, I might not be quite ready for this step," Mathew said. "I need to think and listen, and think some more."

"You have time," the PIE Guy said reassuringly, "especially if you continue your coaching." He turned to Charles, who was waiting to speak, and gestured for him to join the conversation.

"I think I have a pretty good handle on how my leadership style impacts my company vision," Charles began. "And I'm beginning to see a new vision that will include consulting my staff on any changes to our mountain bike product lines. I have a feeling a simple change in my leadership approach is going to have a big impact on employee engagement in my company. I'm going to really enjoy talking to my village about how I can continually improve my leadership as well.

"There are an endless number of productive conversations I can generate about our bikes to extract stories about inspirational mountain bikers at a world-class level, the kind who regularly break stuff and say, 'Faster until the thrill of speed overcomes the fear of death.' Some people in the company are just as passionate about getting families involved in biking as the rest of us when it comes to top-level athletes. Oh, did you see what I did there? I combined personal development, storytelling, and the Donut of Life conversation all in one brief conversation!" he laughed.

"Impressive," the PIE Guy said. "See, it's easy and simple, and it works."

"You mean it's as easy as pie?" Charles said with a charming grin.

"You're on a roll, Charles!" the PIE Guy bellowed as he and the others enjoyed a hearty chuckle.

"But seriously," said Charles, "I understand all of the pieces of the puzzle, but now I need to get back home and begin unpacking this week of great conversations and challenging discussions. I need to engage my village to help me answer questions about the future direction of the company."

"It sounds like you have a plan, Charles," the PIE Guy said. "We still need to hear from you, Nimmi."

"I have a really large network of donors and volunteers, but I've never treated any of them like village members," Nimmi replied. "I know I need to think about them differently and find a better way to share information and to build collaboration. I am tired of trying to pull all the pieces together by myself, all of the time. But every change I think about making seems huge. I don't think I've identified one yet that will be easy enough to accomplish in a reasonable amount of time."

Nimmi continued, "I want to bring some of our supporters on board in a slightly different way. I've been thinking about the commercial value of the relationships we have through our extensive network. This is just one of many ideas, but I'd like to ask a training company to get involved and do pro bono work, and in exchange for their work introduce them to other companies in our network. So in effect, their pro bono payment comes from expanding their network into our village. These introductions could lead to some really exciting collaboration."

"Making those sorts of connections takes strong relationships, which you appear to have. Your challenge is time and prioritization. You mentioned millions of things happening in your head and not enough time to implement them. What one thing can you do differently to build momentum?" the PIE Guy inquired.

"I thought I needed to know 100 percent of my Success PIE ingredients before I could begin," Nimmi stated.

"One step at a time, Nimmi," the PIE Guy interjected. "What were you saying before about resources and taking on too much yourself? How would it work if you were able to articulate your vision and find other people that could help you implement it? This way instead of getting bogged down in the detail of every aspect of what you want to create, you can focus on leading and motivating, and leave the implementing to others."

Nimmi nodded her head. "One step at a time…simple works. I'm beginning to see that I constantly overthink everything and then get bogged down and am unable to act," Nimmi reflected.

"So many people get locked into that pattern," the PIE Guy replied. "So many of us are perfectionists and don't want to make any change until we are 100% ready. But it's simply not required. You can start to communicate and make progress toward success even if you only have 50% of your Success PIE together. The other 50% can be formulated around feedback that comes from discussions with your village."

"You know, Nimmi," Charles said, "I'm going home with only about 20% of my future vision known. The other 80% will require my villagers' help in its creation. I'll facilitate the right discussions to extract that 80% and use it to make progress. I know it will take time, but it's the right thing for me to do, especially when I think about what an engaged workforce can do compared to me driving everything through everyone. Does that help?"

"Thank you, Charles, it certainly does," Nimmi said with a smile. "I need to remember small steps still equal progress and are easier to implement than big steps. The concept that 'simple works' is important to remember, and I don't need to have my vision 100% perfected. Now I know what I am going to do first. I'm going to identify people interested in key areas and approach them to take greater ownership, which in turn requires me to trust them and find better ways to share knowledge with them. If I'm able to do this, I should have higher retention of staff and volunteers.

"In order to do this according to my Success PIE, my P is going to be Preparing a few people to help me in this area, which requires me to change my leadership. I'm going to use my Image—or I—to engage these people and share stories with them about my successes. Then, I'm going to make time—or E for effort—to build their skills and capabilities to enable these people to take on more responsibility in areas in which they feel comfortable.

"My village—in this particular situation—is very small. It will be made up of only a handful of people and maybe a few from external organizations. I'm going to share with them why we need to bring this vision to fruition and see if they are interested in helping make it a reality. I'm going to ask a training company I've been working with to do some pro bono work in exchange for listing them as a partner organization, which will get them exposure with other sponsors and our website visitors.

"The big thing I need to remember is that I can incorporate others into building my vision, and it may actually help build a stronger team and solve a few other problems regarding retention. I need my villagers to help me expand upon it and make it a reality," she concluded. "And to briefly go back to our last session, the 'why' of all this is so I will have time to focus on creating my Volunteer Army, something that's necessary if I want to expand my non-profit beyond its current reach."

"You are a quick study, Nimmi!" the PIE Guy exclaimed.

She smiled. "Like Charles said, this is as easy as PIE. One step at a time, and building a pattern of success really resonates with me. The way you have explained it and broken it down into steps makes it logical and easy to think through. Now, the pieces are falling into place with ease."

"You know what resonates with me?" Toni asked the PIE Guy.

"Not until you tell me," he replied.

"Funny, Mr. PIE Guy," she said. "I see this as an iterative process. Things are always changing, and what I need to share with my village as I grow this market for my unique service will also change. As I change and grow, I'll want to share my successes with my village, and then figure out what I want to work on next. Improvement never stops!"

"What a perfect place to end tonight's session," the PIE Guy said. "You brought up an important point we'll discuss tomorrow: the importance of continually developing. Success isn't a destination, it's a journey. So as we wrap up today's discussion, who would like to recap the day's learning?"

> # Success isn't a destination, it's a journey.

Mathew jumped at the opportunity and said, "One of the best ways to embed learning is to teach others. That's why I jumped at the opportunity to do today's recap. I want to ensure that I know what I need to think about tonight. So, here goes nothing. Our success doesn't happen in a vacuum. People who surround us, whether they are customers, colleagues, bosses, or family and friends, may have contributed to our success. Therefore, we need to include them in our journey, especially when we discover something that may help them, or when we need to give them an update or need their help. Does that about cover it?"

"Outstanding, Mathew, on multiple fronts. You've obviously learned more than you think you did from all those workshops you've attended. Teaching, sharing, or storytelling are good ways to further your understanding of a subject. And the recap of today's chat was spot on! Understanding what your villagers would be interested in hearing about, and identifying the right time to tell them, are important considerations. Thanks for stepping forward to do the recap," the PIE Guy said. "Take a moment or two to capture things that have resonated for you personally today. I'll leave you to ponder and capture your thoughts. Thanks for your efforts today and see you all here tomorrow to wrap up the week on PIE."

CHAPTER 8

KEEP YOUR PIE FRESH

"Strive for continuous improvement,
instead of perfection."

Kim Collins

The following day the PIE Guy's personal development group members returned to Café Creo Prosperitas—but they had more than notebooks and briefcases in hand. The PIE Guy had sent an email that morning asking everyone to bring a few of his or her favorite muffins to share. His reason: You never know where your next great idea will come from. Plus, what's better than a sweet, sticky, crumbly muffin—and a rich cup of coffee, of course—when you're ready to celebrate the last day of a productive learning experience?

"Good morning, everyone," the PIE Guy began. "Today we're going to talk about ways to keep your PIE fresh. If we were discussing a real pie, the best way to do that might be to put it under glass and leave it in the refrigerator. But that's not the case with Success PIE. Personal development requires action if you want to make progress. When we ensure we're progressing with our Success PIE, we're keeping it fresh.

"As you may remember, we talked about the need to avoid the 'paralysis of analysis.' It's not enough to think about the changes you need to make. It's not even enough to write down the things necessary to make those changes. Your Success PIE will be of little benefit until you apply it. Remember, it's action, not intention, that helps people achieve greater success in their lives. While you're applying it, you'll need to review it regularly to ensure it stays relevant and current with the progress you've made.

"Remember back to the beginning of our time together when I shared with you Dr. Greenaway's work on reviewing? He makes it clear that reviewing is important when transforming experiences into an empowering learning process in which development can both enhance and demonstrate the educational potential of life's adventures, including, I believe, our actions and intentions to achieve greater success.

"The review I'm suggesting is easy to use and effective and quick! I call the review 'Smiley Face and 10%,' and it's a tool I've shared with thousands before you, and not always in the context of PIE. It takes only minutes to do—once you get the hang of it—and it will help you keep your PIE fresh.

"Basically, 'Smiley Face and 10%' is a quick review of what you've accomplished and what you need to do a bit better to continue your success trajectory. Here's how it works," the PIE Guy said as he opened his sketchbook and began to draw on a fresh page.

"Draw an oversized 't' on a piece of paper. In the upper left corner of the 't' draw a smiley face. In the upper right corner of the 't' write '10%.' Whatever you do, don't draw a frowning face. A frowning face is very negative, and the sight of it will actually send signals to the part of your brain that produces chemicals that will make you feel even more negative, anxious, and defensive—it's all very complex, but scientifically proven.

"The 10%, on the other hand, does not have the same negative effect on the brain. It represents the things that you can do a bit differently to get a better result. Besides, 10% is similar to the small steps of progress we've been talking about—it's very achievable. You're not asking yourself to do a radical rethink in the middle of your busy life. You're asking yourself what you can do a little bit better. As a result, no nasty defeatist brain chemicals are released, and you'll find yourself moving into 'solution mode,' with your brain doing what it should do—thinking positively about your future.

"Now look at the action items in your Success PIE. Consider each one and ask yourself if you're making the progress you'd like to be making on that particular item. If you are, write that action item under the smiley face column and continue doing the things that have helped you derive success in that particular area.

"If you realize you're not getting the results you want, or you haven't been able to work on an action item, write it under the 10% and move on to the next item in your Success PIE. When you've completed your review, you'll find things to celebrate—those things under the smiley face—and things you can do a little bit more to get a better result—those things under the 10% column.

"Even if you don't yet have any action items listed under the smiley face column, you can celebrate the fact that you've still been devoting time to your personal development. You can then reprioritize the action items in your Success PIE and find ways to build them into your daily schedule," he concluded, closing his sketchbook. "So how are you going to keep your PIE fresh?"

"I'll start," said Stuart. "Your 'Smiley Face and 10%' is so much better than what I was brought up using, and what I use with my guys. Our review often includes what some might consider colorful language, especially when things haven't gone so well. I don't know if I can make the switch to using the nice language you use, but I like the idea."

"As with many of the things we discuss," said the PIE Guy, "it's important to be open enough to listen and then think through what resonates with you and how you would incorporate it into your work or life. Instead of 'Smiley Face and 10%,' you can use different words to describe what you are trying to achieve."

"Like asking 'What went well?' and 'What could have gone better?'" Stuart asked.

"Sure," the PIE Guy replied. "It sounds like you are thinking about using this with your team to engage them in the process of review. I like that. Just by adding 'I,' you can review your own progress on your Success PIE. So how else can you use this tool to keep your PIE fresh?"

Stuart replied, "I think I can share this with my girlfriend as well. We can use it to look at how we're planning our life out together."

"That's excellent," the PIE Guy said. "Your Success PIE can be helpful whenever you make any sort of transition in life—in your case, when you go from being single to being part of a married couple. Eventually, you can use it when transitioning from being a couple to being parents. Review tools like 'Smiley Face and 10%' will keep you on track. I like how you are incorporating PIE into your life. It's certainly a good way to keep your PIE fresh!"

"I'd also like to continue meeting with you about PIE," said Stuart. "But maybe we could do it once a month instead of as an intensive week-long program?"

"We can certainly arrange that type of schedule," the PIE Guy responded. "And how are you going to keep your PIE fresh, Mathew?"

"First off, I must say that this group has been fantastic," Mathew said. "I've learned a lot, but I think I'd like to work on my Success PIE one-on-one. Is that possible? It would certainly be a way to keep my PIE fresh."

"Of course," said the PIE Guy. "While some people find value and get ideas from conversations in a small group, others really like to do a deep dive and discuss Success PIE issues and implementation in a one-on-one session. You mentioned an interest in finding a mentor a few days ago. Reach out to your village and you may find someone—maybe someone at your company—who can serve as that mentor. The important thing is to find the right person for you."

"I will do that," Mathew replied. "Some of the changes I need to make are quite personal and I'd like the opportunity to bounce ideas around with someone who really knows me and my situation. I'm going to set an hour aside once a week to work on my Success PIE. That should also help keep it fresh."

"You can use that expanding village of yours as well," the PIE Guy reminded him.

Clare interjected, "I really like Mathew's idea of setting time aside. The only thing I'm not real clear on is whether or not an hour is enough time to make progress."

The PIE Guy answered, "The time you set aside to keep your PIE fresh is different than the time you set aside to build your Success PIE. It's also different than the time you spend working on implementing your PIE. This time is review time—time to ask yourself what you need to do differently to get a better result with your Success PIE. The review itself takes only minutes, and the remaining time should be devoted to implementing your PIE in the days and weeks to come. Here's another way to build a review into your schedule that I often share to help people make the most effective use of their time. It's based on percentages of 70%, 20% and 10%.

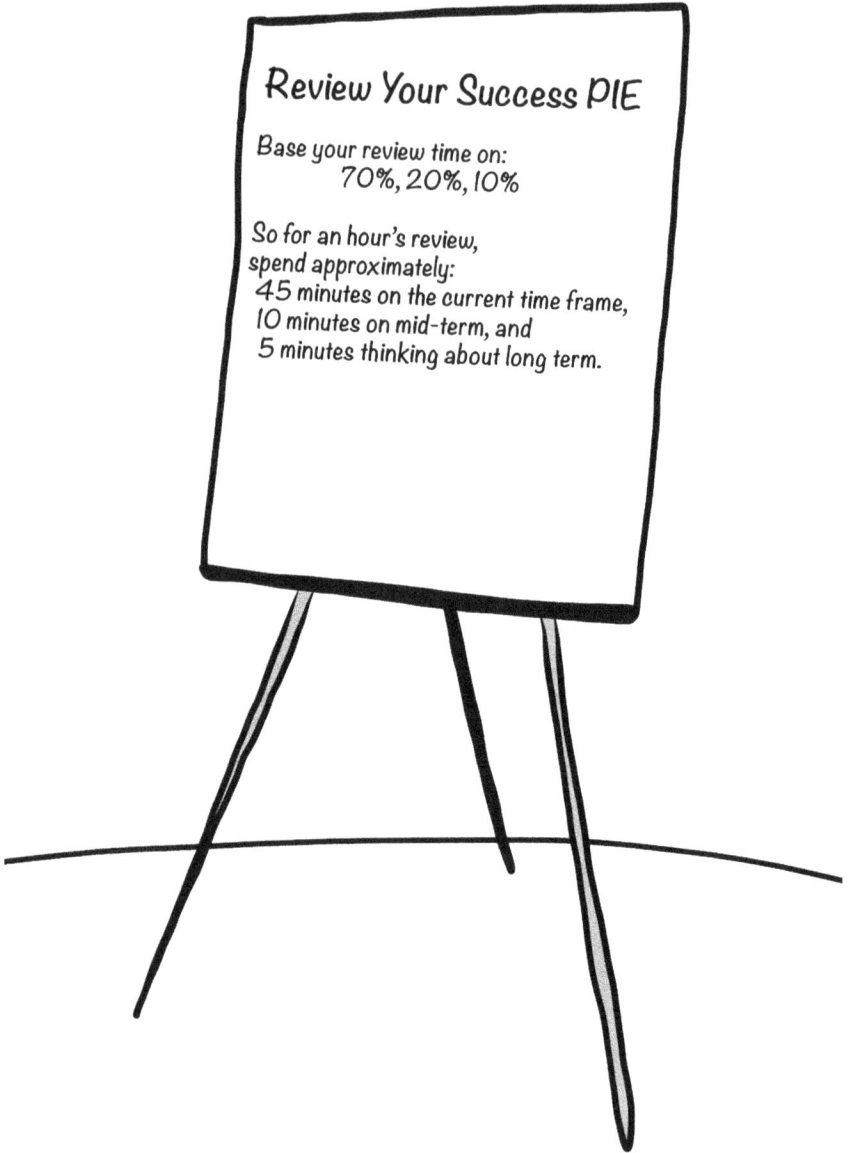

Review Your Success PIE

Base your review time on:
70%, 20%, 10%

So for an hour's review,
spend approximately:
45 minutes on the current time frame,
10 minutes on mid-term, and
5 minutes thinking about long term.

"To ensure your Success PIE doesn't get lost in your computer's documents folder, I suggest reviewing it weekly—or biweekly at the least—and dividing your review time as follows: 70% on what you need to achieve this week or next, 20% on upcoming events/activities in the next month, and 10% on those in the next quarter. If you look at this in terms of one hour, 70% would be roughly 45 minutes, 20% roughly 10 minutes, and 10% five minutes. If you have two hours, or even 30 minutes, you can do the math for that amount of time as well," he explained.

"Got it," said Clare. "So going back to how I'm going to keep my PIE fresh, I will be sharing my Success PIE for starters. This will give others the inside information on what's important to me. It will open my village relationships up for productive conversations. I'm going to start with the easiest members—my husband and family—and then after a bit of feedback, I'll bring my staff into the loop. Finally, I'll share it with the others who have helped me achieve my success to date."

"Those are all great ways to keep your PIE fresh, Clare," said the PIE Guy.

"But I'm not done," she responded. "Once I do this, I'd like to keep this group going. Could we do that? I've got the place and am keen to host the PIE Guy on a regular basis. At least until the group grows too big!"

"Being reminded of your PIE on a daily basis will certainly help your business—in more ways than one," the PIE Guy agreed. "Like a growing village—this village for example—it's a good idea to keep groups small. It's easier to share and learn in small groups. Five to eight is about the right number for a syndicate learning group like the one we've created building your Success PIE. If you're keen, I'm sure we could start a new group right here!" he concluded.

The PIE Guy then seemed to remember something. "Oh, one more thing I should mention—when reviewing your Success PIE using the 70/20/10 tool, it's important to ask yourself if your PIE is still relevant and current. This will require you to think through your work and your life outside of work. Have your personal circumstances changed in a way that would impact your Success PIE? Has your life-stage changed? Has your role changed? Have you changed companies? If you can answer yes to questions like these, you may need to reshape your Success PIE," he concluded.

"I know how I'm going to keep my PIE fresh," Charles said. "I'm going to take the PIE lessons and apply all of them with my direct reports, and then ask them to apply it with their teams. By sharing my Success PIE, I can check for relevancy with my village. Because I understand the value of an engaged team and village, and because I am working on and becoming more comfortable leading through my vision without diving into the details, I'll ask the questions and build a current strategy that uses the thoughts, ideas, and energy from my team."

"It always amazes me to see how many variations there are to make this simple PIE concept work!" the PIE Guy exclaimed. "That's wonderful, Charles, and that is exactly what development is all about. Share the good things that make you more successful, and watch your village grow. It's amazing to experience. Check in with us when you are back home and let us know how you are getting along."

"It's a shame we can't keep this going," Charles responded. "It would be nice to keep it rolling, but I can't because of the distance. As you know, I live in Scotland."

"There are formal and informal ways to keep your PIE fresh," the PIE Guy assured him. "We have a virtual community that you can connect with. Or you could start your own Success PIE group in Scotland. You won't have the lovely muffins of Café Creo Prosperitas to munch on, but you will still be connected."

"I think the online community will be perfect for me," Toni said. "Virtual meetings work great with my schedule. But I also want to share what I've learned and start a PIE group within my organization. I'll find a way to use social media to connect with my growing network and convert more of my network into village members. That will keep my Success PIE fresh!"

"There are so many ways to keep your PIE fresh," the PIE Guy said. "Toni, you've learned so much, and you have a great following. Don't forget to review your Success PIE regularly. Your brain works so fast, and you have so many things going on, it would be easy to turn all of your attention to the next objective. How are you going to check to see if your Success PIE is remaining relevant and current?"

"I actually already thought about this," Toni replied. "In light of all I've learned, I realize there are some things that I will never be good at, and I'm okay with that. There is someone in my organization who always keeps me honest, so I'm going to engage her in my vision first so she can help keep me on track. She will also love the new language I'll be using when reviewing projects based on your 'Smiley Face and 10%,' and I'm not going to change a word!"

"Fantastic, Toni," the PIE Guy said. "I'm always at the end of an email if you need help. Now what about you, Nimmi? How will you keep your PIE fresh?"

"When we began the session today, I was thinking about how simple this all is…almost too simple," Nimmi replied. "But then I realized that is what you've been saying all along, simple works. It doesn't mean that 'I am simple' or that we need simple things because we are not clever. We need simple things in our complex lives, full stop.

"When we make development too complex, it most likely won't work. An example of this was yesterday when I didn't really 'get it' until I thought through what people were saying and adapted the information into something that worked for me. From there it all clicked. I have a bit of work to do prioritizing the things I want to achieve, because many of them require changes in my behavior before I will be able to attain more with my team.

"One of the ways I'll keep my PIE fresh is to include my core village and share the lessons learned from this workshop. I'll tell them how I will benefit from them asking me about progress in specific areas. They can help hold me accountable. That's easy and doesn't cost a thing, and I'll share what I've learned during these sessions!

"The other way is to build a review into my schedule every other week to see how well I am working my Success PIE. The 'Smiley Face and 10%' tool fits in with the softer approach I often use at my work. It doesn't do any good getting upset about progress that isn't achieved at the pace that one expects. By using this 'Smiley Face and 10%' tool, I see that it even offers me the ability to celebrate the small steps I'm able to take and keeps me on track.

"This should take me a few months. Then I am going to work on the second round of my Success PIE. As I learn the process, I'll be able to achieve more with an engaged village. I may need to connect with Charles every once in a while to compare notes on facilitating to gain engagement, and on being okay with 20% of my vision as an unknown.

"Also, by taking small chunks of development, and achieving success more regularly and by reviewing and rebuilding my Success PIE, I should have a very relevant and current Success PIE," she concluded.

"Another way to keep your PIE fresh is by staying in contact with the people in this group and continuing to learn from each other," the PIE Guy offered. "Well done, Nimmi. You've taken to this like a duck to water."

The PIE Guy stood for a good stretch.

"We've covered a lot in the past week. Let's take a moment to appreciate all that we've achieved," he said. "You've discovered your version of PIE: Preparedness, Image, and Effort. You've examined the importance of your village and why the people in your village are linked to your success. You have ways to identify key village members, and you know why it's essential to communicate your PIE to them. We've talked about the criticality of reviewing your progress with the 'Smiley Face and 10%,' and we've discussed the many ways in which you can keep your PIE fresh.

"I'm confident you are all well on your way to making your Success PIE work for you. I want you to remember to smile and celebrate every step of the way. Remember, simple works, and Success PIE is as easy as pie to implement.

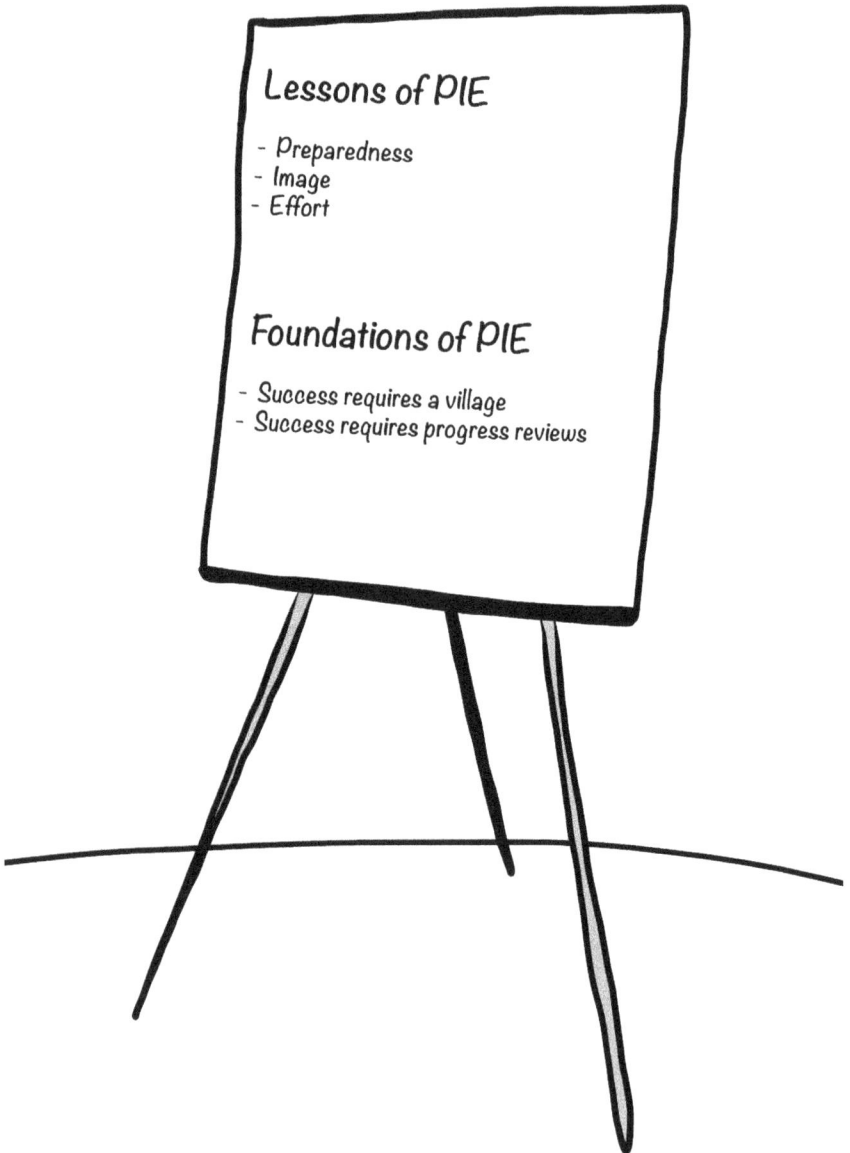

Lessons of PIE

- Preparedness
- Image
- Effort

Foundations of PIE

- Success requires a village
- Success requires progress reviews

"I also want you to remember that change is an opportunity to embrace, not a burden to run away from. Focus on challenges over which you have influence, and strive for productive conversations. You can learn lessons from the past, but it's important to live in the present and look toward the future.

"Finally, remember that you must 'keep the oven on.' When you finish one Success PIE, it's time to mix up another batch. Until that time, remember to keep your PIE fresh." And with a swirl of his cape, the PIE Guy was gone.

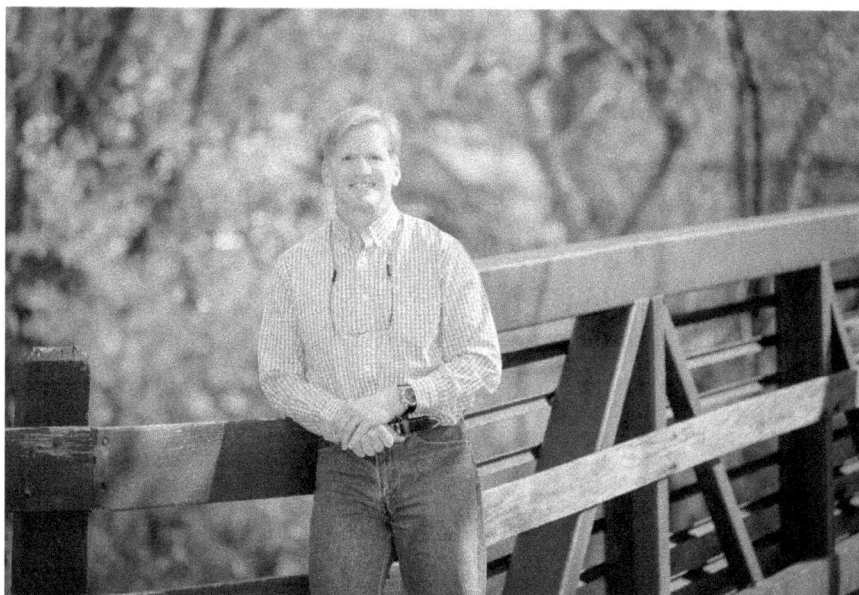

©Jeff Warner PHOTOGRAPHIC

ABOUT THE AUTHOR

Todd Arthur Heskett is passionate about the people side of change management. He has spent more than a decade helping people achieve 10% greater success in the corporate sector and in more than 30 nations around the world. He has lived outside his home country for almost 15 years. His clients are found in *Fortune's Global 100*, *Interbrand's Best Retail Brands*, and *The World's Most Valuable Brands* by *Forbes*. He works with an extraordinary range of outstanding achievers, including global leaders, country heads, leaders of organizations, leaders of not-for-profits, and government agencies.

Todd has addressed distinguished audiences ranging from Society of Human Resource Management to the Leadership Investment. He regularly gives back to his local community volunteering his time helping non-profits with change programs. A key component of writing this book is to expand his reach to people that normally do not have access to executive coaching or cutting-edge learning and development in their organizations.

Todd's passion for improving by 10% is deeply rooted in his life, his family, and his activities outside of work. You may not see him on an Olympic roster, but you will see him improving in everything he does, whether rock climbing, mountain biking, inspiring his children, or finding new ways to enhance his marriage. He believes improving by 10% is an amazingly simple concept that has transformed his life. His inspirational talks, like his book, *Keep Your PIE Fresh*, outline a simple approach to help find and achieve 10% greater success.

Remember, development ALTERS success.
ALTERS = Act. Learn. Think. Elevate. Repeat. Share.

To unlock your potential contact Todd directly at:
Todd.Heskett@Watermarq-Consulting.com

Todd Heskett is the Founder and Managing Partner of Watermarq and has been setting people up for success since 2001

To learn more about Watermarq's web-based coaching support system and smartphone application called Ripple, or to become a coaching client, send Todd an email at Todd.Heskett@Watermarq-Consulting.com

Remember: Development ALTERS Success
ALTERS = Act. Learn. Think. Elevate. Repeat. Share.